G000163137

Deconstructing Motivation

How to Effortlessly Motivate
Yourself to Do Anything in Life

ANDREW ALEXANDER

ISBN: 9781096090168
Independently published

DEDICATION

I wrote this book for the same person I wrote all my other books for. You. I love you more than anything in this world and you deserve nothing but the best in this life.

-Andrew Alexander, July 2019

CONTENTS

ONLINE VIDEO TRAINING PROGRAM

If you're interested in learning more about reaching peak performance levels and being able to maintain lasting motivation in your personal and professional life, please visit the following website to access our premium video training program and/or coaching.

www.DeconstructingMotivation.com

Chapter 1

Painful Beginnings

THE MOMENT WHERE CHANGE BEGINS

I'm Sorry, But This is Going to Be Painful

I'm not sure if you're ready to do what I'm about to ask you to do. It's going to be painful, you're most likely going to cry, and it's going to suck at first. But I can promise you that things are going to be a thousand times more painful in the future if you don't do what I'm asking you to do right now. The reason why it's so important that you do this right now, today...

Somewhere in the world, a man who smoked cigarettes his entire life was just diagnosed with lung cancer during a routine checkup at his doctor's office. The man has a wife, three children, and financial responsibilities to take care of them all.

The doctor just gave him three months to live.

Sitting there on the table feeling naked in his underwear, the grown man breaks down in tears rolling down his face.

Every emotion you could possibly expect to feel in this dark moment came rushing to the surface all at once. The fear of what might happen to his family when he's gone.

Will they be able to afford the expensive mortgage payments without him? How will they pay for car insurance, college tuition, and food? Will they even be able to survive?

It's already too late.

Knowing that all of his life, he told himself he should quit smoking; but decades later, he never actually did what he said he was going to do.

He's now in shock and crying uncontrollably with the feeling of remorse and regret.

The nurse in the hallway hears his gasps of pain and stops in her tracks as her head goes down in despair, knowing the man just got the bad news. She lets out a deep breath of sorrow and continues to walk on to her next patient.

As the man leaves the doctor's office shell-shocked, in a trance-like state, he gets to his car and sees the cigarette butt on the ground next to the driver's side door.

That was the last cigarette the man would ever smoke in his entire life.

The pack of Marlboros resting on his center console was no longer an instinctual habit where he "reaches over and lights up a smoke" but instead is now a painful reminder of his impending death. The sight that used to be so normal to him now brings up so much pain and agony which twists a knot in his stomach.

What's he going to do now?

It's already too late.

If he could only look back in time and scream to a younger version of himself: "Quit that bad habit now! It's not something you should be doing!"

But what's the problem with that?

People have been saying this to him his entire life. He said he was going to change his ways on many occasions. He tried to give up countless times before. He logically knew what he should be doing. The information has been there all along. The problem he faced is that He. Wasn't. Actually. Doing. It.

So why, after years of knowing this, did his behavior finally change in this moment?

If you can answer that question, you'll understand motivation at its core.

But first, let's get you started…

Why Are You Here?

You're here because you want to do something in your life. What's that one specific goal you set out for yourself, that, if you achieve it, it would make reading this book completely worth it? What have you been procrastinating on in the past? Do you want to build a business and experience the freedom of being an entrepreneur? Do you want to improve your health by eating better and getting back in shape? Do you want to publish a book of your own someday? Perhaps you're after the relationship and dating life of your dreams so you want to build up the motivation and confidence to make it happen. Or is it something else? What is it that you're working towards that will make this book worth reading from start to finish?

What is it that you committed to take action towards, so when you finally achieve this goal, you can look back and say that Deconstructing Motivation was the thing that made it work? I wrote this book for those of us who are actually doing the things most people want to do; but always say they are going to do it "someday". Those are the people who continue to remain stuck in place.

This book started as a personal journey.

March 2012: Rock Bottom Sets You Free

You see, for the first 25 years of my life, I've been a chronic procrastinator. I used to always put things off until last minute, was forced by deadlines at work and school that other people had to keep me accountable for. If I didn't do my homework on time, I would fail the class. If I didn't do the work I had to do, I would lose my job.

I had my personal goals in life to start my own business and to get back in shape, but after a certain point, I really let myself go and things started to slip. I didn't have the same motivational systems in place that kept me dependent on those training wheels of school and corporate structure my entire life. What I truly lacked was the self-motivation to do things on my own. Subconsciously waiting for somebody else to give me permission to act and keep me accountable. That person never came and my goals continued to remain as dreams in my mind.

Instead, my life was filled with bad habits that had me functioning like a zombie in auto-pilot. I would get out of bed drowsy and exhausted after 3 snoozes of the alarm clock, start my day off with a large fattening and greasy meal from the various fast food restaurants on the way to the nearly-minimum wage job I hated. Too tired, drained, busy, exhausted, and full of excuses as to why I didn't have the time to work on my goals at night. But I always found time for browsing the internet and having fun with my friends. I always found the time for the things I knew I shouldn't be doing. Being motivated is more than simply doing the things we have to do. It's also about identifying and cutting out the things we should stop. Learning the skills to build the confidence that we can actually achieve this goal in the first place. Having the proper belief systems, external environment, and priorities in life to ensure we are aligned with the right track. The ability to deal with uncertainty, fears, failure, and adversity along the way; without letting it get us discouraged and stop in our tracks. There is a complex structure of human motivation, and this book allows you to begin untying the knot.

I was always suffering from my own insecurities and social anxiety that held me back from having the relationships I wanted. But the thing that really did it for me was when I was 25 years old, broke, unemployed, and living in my parent's retirement home for two years after college; 600 miles away from all of my friends. I couldn't even afford to pay for food or housing on my own. Covering up the pain with a serious junk food addiction, this eventually led me to hit a rock bottom where life got so bad things couldn't get any worse. So I was forced to change. All too often, people in this life don't go about being motivated to make serious changes until it's already too late.

Do you know how you often follow the same routines day after day? Without some type of external event to shock the system, it's hard to notice that you've been caught in a holding pattern for so long. Our bodies are naturally programmed to conserve resources and survive, but what about those of us who want to grow and thrive?

So how do you break free and enter the pattern of better habits, motivation, and actually achieving your stated goals?

I'll tell you what doesn't work: I would spend my days dreaming of a better future. I would see these entrepreneurs on the internet build businesses that allowed them to earn millions of dollars per year, passive income, and they had the freedom to travel the world, drive exotic sports cars, and live in nice mansions. The experiences they had in this life were extraordinary. So I decided to give it a go. In all areas of my life. I tried one of those 30-day diet challenges where I eventually gave up after eating an entire bag of potato chips for breakfast on day two. I taught myself how to code websites, I read a lot of books on business, and often found myself giving up when I didn't see any results right away. I was always jumping from one idea to another when I didn't have any quick success. In the business world, they call it shiny object syndrome. Something is always going to look more appealing when you face a setback or struggle with what you're currently doing. But where most people jump ship, only the truly motivated and the truly committed push forward towards one clear destination through even the hardest of times. These are the ones who make it to the promised land on the other side. It took me years to learn that lesson the hard way.

You see, I had access to all the information and steps that could get me there. The same skills used by people who achieved a life like that. But the missing piece of the puzzle that was holding me back from **doing**, was the long-term sustained, self-motivation that keeps people pushing forward through even their greatest setbacks and periods of laziness/uncertainty. I wanted to build the positive habits that would make motivation a new part of my life that I could finally enjoy living.

The Formula for Human Motivation

To be honest, it wasn't a quick win after I made the decision to figure out what it takes to be motivated for myself. I struggled with doing the wrong things for many years. It wasn't until later when I learned that, behind the goals we all set out for ourselves, there is a deeper structure of human behavior. A formula. By evolution, or design, all human bodies and minds are programmed with an algorithm that dictates exactly how we behave.

What I learned is that bad habits are not 'bad' habits at all. They are a system of behaviors that serve the exact function it needs within that system. Left-over old programing that can be changed with new behaviors that align with your current goals. So that's what this book is about; better understanding this algorithm so we can use it to our advantage. To utilize the existing structure of our bodies to lead us effortlessly on the right track towards doing the things we once used to hate doing. And that's where my journey began; struggling for years on end and being unmotivated to achieve my goals. Dreaming.

Where will it lead you?

Fast forward seven years later, as I'm writing this book for you in a coffee shop in some South American coastal city, I'm traveling the world today. Using this formula for motivation, I built three businesses impacting the lives of over 1.3 million people, published multiple books, built over 20 mobile apps in less than half a year, lost 50 pounds in three months (without even trying to lose weight), motivated myself to improve my dating life and attract a woman who loves me as much as I love her.

While there are a lot of tactics and skills out there to make all of this happen (diet plans, fitness routines, sales training, etc.), that's like giving somebody a cookbook with the exact recipe and ingredients to cook their favorite dish; only for them to sit at the dinner table waiting for it to be cooked for them. This is the book about how to actually start doing it and to start applying the things you've learned in the real world.

After I began my Deconstructing Motivation journey, I mustered up the motivation to overcome my fears and quit the corporate world at the age of 27 so I could live out my dreams of traveling all across the United States, Europe, and South America for five years straight. One year I was feeling inspired after watching a motivational video of someone traveling the world (never thinking it would be possible for me). The next year, I was the one traveling the world and making those videos myself.

Motivation is a powerful thing.

It gives you the ability to accomplish really great things in a rather short period of time. But more importantly it provides you with a full understanding of human behavior. This allows you to have better control of your emotions as well as be more influential and empathetic in your communication with others. If you work in sales, marketing, or any other customer-facing job; knowing why people behave the way they do gives you power.

So if you're sick and tired seeing other people do the things you should be doing with ease, thinking they got lucky, seeing how they had it easier than you, dreaming of the day when you can finally live a life like that...You're going to have to get off your butt and start doing the things you need to do to get there. It's a long journey you're going to have to walk, so you might as well get started today.

It feels so much better when you're actually doing these things for yourself. The security, comfort, contribution, and accomplishment you feel **while doing the things** you used to hate doing is a million times more powerful than the hypnotic trance you get stuck in from mindlessly browsing through pictures on social media, waking up with a hangover from partying, or binge watching Netflix. Do you notice how those things seem to subtly drain you of your energy?

The things you used to avoid (hard work, new difficult tasks, exercise, healthy eating) are seen through a whole new perspective of growth, accomplishment, and achievement. The feelings you get from being in the flow are out of this world! When you filter through the noise, there is a clean Zen-like state that serves as the immediate gratification you've always been striving for. I'll talk more about that very powerful point later in this book.

So here I am, at the age of 32, baffled about how someone like me who struggled with procrastination his entire life was able to accomplish so much in such a short period of time. And grateful that I had to pull out of one of my worst rock-bottoms in terms of motivation ever; to realize that whatever you want to achieve (with the right persistence, hard work, and failure along the way), is possible for you. So dream a little bit bigger, commit to something you believe in, and make this motivational journey worthwhile to you.

What Makes Deconstructing Motivation Unique?

Motivational videos pump you up with feel-good emotions that quickly fade away. Deconstructing Motivation is really about the deeper structure of how the human body is programmed to behave. Regardless of the surface-level thing you want to be motivated to do, there is a psychology and biology that dictates how all humans are programmed to act. In this book, you will learn all about that. Why do we do certain things when we say we want to do something else? Why do we avoid some tasks? Why do continue to partake in the habits we have no matter how self-destructive we know they are for our life? How do we shock our system and break free from our old ways, taking on a more motivated way of being in this life? Leaving those old bad habits in the past; lost, and gone forever.

If you think of the human mind and body as a computer,

there's mental programming (algorithms) we are born with as survival mechanisms to keep us alive. If you fall into a campfire, the algorithm has a script that gets your body in motion to jump out and run away. Can you see in this instance of the campfire you don't need willpower to stick with it and be motivated? The human body's natural emotions kick in and you just get things done!

Now, imagine if exercising or working on your big goals were just as easy. Where it would take a lot of willpower for you to NOT be working on your goals, instead of trying to keep willpower to make you actually start doing those things in the first place.

In addition to the mental programing and algorithms we were born with, there are other scripts we've programmed ourselves with along the way based on our experiences. Past emotional traumas cause us to avoid doing certain things. Don't put your hand on the hot stove more than once. You learned your lesson when you did it once and it's imprinted into your DNA. Have you ever faced rejection when you asked out someone you like or been cursed out on a sales call? Felt the pain? Just like the hot stove lesson, this imprint on your DNA has a lasting impact on your behavior until you learn how to change it. An emotional blockage stops you in your tracks.

Another example of the algorithm behind human behavior at its deepest form: If you're hungry, there is an algorithm for instinctually supplying yourself with food. Even a newborn baby can do it without thinking about it.

You know the old saying "Sex Sells" and there are advertisements everywhere with attractive women and men showing their skin? It doesn't matter if they are holding a bottle of cologne or a plant-based vegan cheeseburger in their hands. The programming of the human body needing to reproduce is one that is written to ensure the survival of the human species. Can you see how there is an algorithm already there? This is why the sexual drive desire is so powerful. Without any motivation or willpower, we are magnetically attracted to move towards it! It's an energetic force within us that does the work effortlessly. Whether it's to reproduce and ensure the survival of the human race, eat meals, preserve our body, or one of the other 16 drivers of all human behavior; it's this deeper structure of emotional drivers that is responsible for doing the things we do. This algorithm is so powerful that no matter how much restraint you have when you try to hold back, there is no stopping you from doing it!

Now, imagine instead of trying to force yourself to do things, going against your natural drivers of human behavior; you understand exactly how it works, and you can plug the things you need to do within this formula so you can work alongside it and harness the full potential of its force. It's like utilizing the power of a river's current while paddling your kayak downstream instead of franticly trying to move your way up against the current, quickly to get burnt out, overwhelmed, and feeling stuck!

It doesn't matter what your goals are in this life, the structure is the same. Please take that lesson away and apply this formula to anything you want.

It is with my intent that by the time you fully understand human behavior through this book, you can simply plug in your desired goal, have the pre-built algorithm take over, and allow your body's natural programming to run its course. This way, motivation to achieve your goals is simply a chain reaction of taking the first step and effortlessly pulling you all the way through the finish line. So you can sit back, relax, and enjoy the ride!

This is a book about understanding all that. But I'd like to start off this book with the most powerful force of human behavior known to man...

Chapter 2

A Limitless Source of Unbreakable Energy

IF SOMETHING IS IMPORTANT ENOUGH TO YOU, PAIN, FAILURE, AND OBSTACLES WILL NEVER SLOW YOU DOWN OR HOLD YOU BACK

If you're going on a road trip, you're going to need fuel to put the vehicle in motion. If the automobile is the metaphorical representation of your body, your emotions are the fuel that flows through it in order get you going. Most people who struggle with motivation are complacent where they are, filled with apathy, don't feel the burn, and have no strong emotional desire to do something. The car is running on fumes because their energy is being drained elsewhere. Other people find short-term motivation that gets them excited to begin something but it never pulls them all the way through to the finish line. They rev up the engine real loud in the beginning, speed up real fast, and on the outside they act all excited; but they quickly burn through the fuel they have, which is never sustained and lasting in nature. Short sprints and periods of burnout don't win the long-term race. But inside each and every one of us is a source of power that is undying and limitless in nature.

Once you tap into this power, you can fuel yourself all the way from start to finish in order to maintain sustained motivation through even the hardest of times. Even if you move forward with a 99.9% chance of failure, you still do it because what you're about to tap into is more important than anything else in this world.

At the core of your being is the deepest force of desire in our entire lives. This is the thing we live for. That one thing that is more important to us than anything else in the world. Do you ever notice that there's one thing that continues to bring up your emotions time after time? That no matter how difficult, how impossible, or how far-away this is, you can't seem to shake it? As I mentioned in the last chapter, a caveman puts his hand in a hot campfire; and what happens? The emotions fill his neurology and it automatically puts his body into motion. But what happens when the pain is gone and he's back to his default way of life? That same motivation is short-lived and gone.

Now imagine that instead of having to stop and refuel at a gas station, there is an unlimited source of fuel that is created from within...

Your Core Desire

In spiritual teachings they say that deep down inside us is the infinite power of the universe. Visualize that when you move past your conscious mind, even deeper than your unconscious, there is a portal that opens up and a limitless amount of energy from a higher realm is already within you. When you open up the flood gates, this energy begins to come out, flow through you, and get released out into the world.

Whatever you decide to do with this energy is your decision to make. For many of the people who haven't experienced this yet, it's often times blocked and suppressed deep down within. Because they don't feel it at the surface, they go looking externally for motivation, instead of within themselves. When we remove all the obstacles and blocks that prevent us from connecting with who we are at the core and why we are here; this opens up a flow state energy that just lets the motivation naturally occur. In more practical terms, this is how athletes "Get in the Zone" and writers such as myself "Get into Flow State". A clean wave of energy just flows through us. Tapping into flow state is a story for a whole other book in itself, but trust me when I say this…Inside each and every one of us; it's already there. Stop looking for things outside of you to be the source of your motivation. It will be a struggle and often times short lived. Whether you believe in the spiritual use of my words or not, simply view it as a visual representation to clearly see that there is an internal source of motivation that doesn't require any external factors to inspire us. And when you find out what that is for you, it's a very powerful thing.

Start with Why

I began Deconstructing Motivation by asking why you are here. What's important to you? There is this old motivational book by Simon Sinek that talks about your "Why". Why are you doing the things you say you need to be doing? This is much different than What you need to do or How you will do it. If you think of the What as the specific road you drive on and the How as the car you're in, the Why is the fuel that moves you. Without your Why, you are stuck in place. An example for fitness, in reverse order, would be as follows:

- **How am I doing it?** I am waking up every morning and going for an hour long walk by the beach.
- **What am I doing?** I am losing weight.
- **Why am I doing it?** I want to ensure my body lives a long and healthy life so I can enjoy my experiences with the woman I love and have a clean flow of energy for my mission and purpose in this life.

Can you see in this example that the How and the What are just empty vehicles without any energetic fuel to get the vehicle in motion? When you talk about your Why, you should feel the emotions come up in your body as a sign that you know it's here. Can you imagine a white flow of energy come out of you so you can channel this energy through many outlets in order to get the results you want? I want to enjoy my experiences with the one I love, so my Why is the stream that flows through my books. Through the video programs I create and the coaching sessions I offer. So, what's the most important thing in the world for you?

What's your Why?

Channel Your Energy

Now, think of the things you need to be doing. Is it something meaningful enough to you (your passion)? Or is it something you have to force yourself to do and it's a struggle like homework in a pointless class you're required to take? Or is it something you know you need to do in order to get to a goal you actually want to achieve (you have to run to get in shape)? If you don't have the right reasons for doing something, motivation will be a struggle. There are many paths that lead to the top of the mountain. When you figure out Why you want to do these things, you're at the starting point to fill your body up with the emotions that are this unbreakable motivational force.

I'll be completely honest here. Even after you find out what this is, you have to make a conscious effort tap into this source and use it. To really connect with the core of your emotions and then channel that energy into what you do. It's a very subtle distinction, and for many people who have emotional blocks in life (we all do); it could take months to work through them in order to really narrow down what it is. As you prepare to get into action mode, it takes a conscious effort and a reminder to use it. What I stated just now are my own interpretations and personal experiences I've had after reading his book.

Utilizing Your Why for Business

Applying this principle to sales and marketing, he says that people don't buy What you do or How you do it. They are magnetically drawn in because of Why you do it. I have one friend who was starting his own business. He invented a stylish line of fitness apparel that he was so passionate about. Every time he spoke about his product, he was radiating with passion and excitement. This magnetic force seemed to just pull customers in. A few years later, he was doing just over $250,000 in sales. I didn't even really care for the What he was doing, but his Why was so powerful and radiant, it drew me in and I supported him anyway. It's magnetic. For my entrepreneur friends reading this: I know a lot of savvy business owners say you can't sell a product with passion alone, and they are partially right. But with the right mix of having this Why and a product people enjoy paying for; something special happens with your motivation because of that. But more importantly, this fuel serves as an unbreakable force that pulls you through even the hardest of times so you can arrive at your destination on the other side after many people give up. After a trail lined with 1,000 failures is where you find success. What's compelling enough to pull you along on that journey so you not only get started but never stop when things get difficult on your way? In the times where most people get discouraged and give up, Billionaire Elon Musk has a famous quote, "When something is important enough, you do it even if the odds are not in your favor."

At the start of my motivational journey, I didn't know what it was but I began seeing it time and time again, learning that it comes from the bottom of your heart. And then one day, it was there.

A Cause You Believe In

Some of my closest friends are passionate animal rights activists who go out into the world day in and day out to fight for the freedom of the animals they love. Not just dogs and cats, but chickens, cows, and pigs as well. This comes from the belief system that all living beings are born equal and deserve life. From holding up signs on the side of highways in freezing cold temperatures, to handing out flyers on college campuses; some of them are even facing felony charges as a result of breaking into animal agriculture facilities to expose the horrific environment and illegal practices that go on inside. At the risk of their own health, safety, and personal freedom; they are motivated to always be pushing forward by the compassion in their hearts. How does your motivation compare to that? Are you really that committed?

For months on end, I joined them. I mustered up the motivation to get out in sub-zero temperatures and hold signs/hand out flyers promoting the cause. But that motivation to move towards this shared goal was short lived. My Why was fueled through another How. Instead of activism, I currently am a partner in a vegan food company. I have a passion to help people build healthier eating habits. I don't break into factory farms to protest for animal rights. I support what they are doing, but it's not my path. I deliver healthy plant-based meals that are easier to eat and more delicious than even fast food restaurants or meat alternatives.

What lights a fire in one person's heart may be slightly different than what gets another person going on a similar path. With both of our goals being equal, my Why and their Why have a different outlet of flow. Think of having an infinite pool of energy inside of you, at the deepest level, and it flows in a certain direction towards the purpose you serve. Flow with it and you'll be aligned. Flow against it and you'll feel resistance. Find your Why, tap into the flow state, and motivation becomes a breeze.

Imagine that your "Why" is the gravitational center of a black hole propelling everything around it. It's the one thing that everything in your universe is revolving around. It's that deeply-rooted passion and desire in the bottom of your heart. It's the one thing in life you can't escape. You don't choose it. You feel it in your heart, from the deepest level of your being.

If you're faced with apathy, lack of motivation, hopelessness, or God forbid you're still caught up in the trap of doing the things in life other people (family, society, etc.)

expect you to be doing; these things are simply layers of the onion that will one day soon start to peel away until you find out what is truly there in the center.

Finding Out What It Is

Some things you have to do in life may not be directly connected to your Why. But there is a way to connect your Why with those things so you can effortlessly enjoy doing them as well. Learn to find things interesting and you'll never be bored. Even through your darkest days of failure where everything goes wrong as well as physical rock bottoms in life; it's that tiny pinhole of light shining through the black fabric of the universe way off into the distance. It's that feeling deep down that one day you know **it's going to happen**. Before thinking about it, what answer comes to mind when you ask yourself, "If money wasn't an issue, what is it that I want to be doing?". If nothing comes up, meditate on a similar question, "If money wasn't an issue, what would I want to be doing; for others?" and you'll be one step closer to it. What means a lot to you? Is there a something you would go after anyway even if you had a 100% chance of failure and all the forces in the universe say it's never going to ever happen?

Fear & Failure Become Irrelevant

When you are living your Why, you don't need motivation because if something is important enough to you – you will go through hell and back and face the prospect of death itself in order to make it happen. When your Why is strong enough, you would rather move forward, give it everything you have, and fail miserably only to never achieve the goal; than to die one day without even trying in the first place. That's when you know you have it.

When you set goals that are so-so and are not important enough to you, this leaves room for fearing failure. The things you've learned in this chapter are a way to make desire trump failure every single time so you'll do nothing but push forward to achieve it. Anything else that gets in the way will become completely irrelevant. What is it for you?

Why Am I Writing This Book?

Part of it is to help other people more easily navigate the struggles I once used to face with procrastination. Many people have a driving force to help people through struggles they've once faced in the past or to remove problems that currently exist in their own life. Many people enjoy the flow of energy that comes through them in an artistic form (writing, art, singing, or dance). Helping people achieve their goals is part of my motivation that just flows out of me.

But the burning passion and desire in my heart is to be with the woman I love. To create the complete financial freedom and abundance to provide both of us with the most amazing and remarkable experiences in this life. To be able to travel the world together. To be in love and feel that deep-sense of ultimate trust and connection. To embark on new, rich, adventures together. To acquire the resources for doing great things that impact other people's lives and the world for the better. It's that unbreakable magnetic force that always drives me to her. And I channel this energy from my heart through my books, my programs online, my YouTube videos, and my coaching. To help people break free from the life they feel stuck in so they too can live the life of their dreams. I have learned over the years that all people are capable of achieving so much more than they can imagine. It pains my heart to see them settle for less and live limited lives they feel stuck in. There's a way to escape.

What you're reading now are not simply words on paper. They are my energy, transmitted through my fingertips, into the words you are experiencing now.

If you think of my personal goal as the top of the mountain, and the desire to share that life I described with the woman I love, that energy from that love is what fuels my body to climb to the top without giving up.

1. It's one thing to do my work that eventually leads to a result of my goals with her (not a direct flow).
2. But it's a much more powerful thing to channel this energy through my work, directly for her. Helping

her through a problem in her life, and then sharing it with the world (a direct flow of energy).

There's a difference, and to be honest, both work for motivation. Think about how you can look past my surface-level examples, see the burning fuel of the business owner and animal rights activists, and use these same principles to apply to what you're doing in your life.

Your Why Doesn't Have to Be the Goal. It's the fuel. What's serving a purpose for me will most certainly be different for you. As you can see, my love for her is my Why. I don't need to motivate myself to do anything to be pulled to her. But for my professional life, I channel that energy and the fuel through an outlet (books/business) that brings me closer to this life I am building for her.

It took me many years to find this. I had to crawl through the swamps and pull myself out of deep dark places to finally know what it is. And you will too. It's a normal part of the discovery process on this long journey we call life. All the answers you need will certainly not pop up all of a sudden. Embrace the long-term journey to get there. But once you truly fill your heart with Why you are doing what you are doing – it's a magnetic motivational force that will take over and just like jumping out of a hot campfire, you won't even have to feel like you're working hard to get there. Motivation comes naturally with the fuel inside of you that never runs out and continues to burn forever.

Most motivation you've experienced up until this point in life will be short-lived. Like a car that constantly runs out of fuel and you have to push it to gas station to fill it up again. That motivation is how many people achieve their goals. They setup a motivational system in place that works for them. And that same system may work best for you.

This chapter is just one option of many ways to motivate yourself on this Deconstructing Motivation journey we are on. The following chapters of the book will give you more. **Why do you do what you do?** Feel it from the center of your chest because it comes from the heart. And notice how this source is never-ending.

Conclusion

So while you move forward with Deconstructing Motivation, rest assured that the processes I share with you today are not only from my own personal experience, trials, errors, failures, and successes. From mentorship by some of the smartest psychologists, peak performance coaches, and experts in human behavior on this planet. Millionaire entrepreneurs, celebrities, social media influencers, and athletes have all hired me for my services. From the hundreds of personal coaching clients I've worked with one-on-one, and the thousands of emails I've sent over the years to help people be more motivated and to achieve their goals in life. Through this book, I Deconstructed Motivation into a formula that you can start to use today. While I have many trainings and a few fancy certificates I can put on the wall of my office to impress clients, this is a book less about theory and more from real world human experience; and stories I can share. It is my pleasure and my honor to share with you the formula I learned so you can do the same, regardless of where your starting point is or what your specific goals are. Whatever YOUR goals are, dig beneath the surface and understand Why you do the things you do. In a few chapters, we'll walk you through an Outcome-Based Goal Setting process so you can be crystal clear on what you should be putting your energy into. It will give you a clear direction so you can know where to get going from there. But next, let me warn you about the traps you may face along the way. I sincerely hope that a new chapter of your life starts right now, today.

- Andrew Alexander, Author of this book.

More Books. Supplemental Video Programs.
Results-Driven Coaching.

www.DeconstructingMotivation.com

Chapter 3

Dopamine Traps

A FALSE SENSE OF ARTIFICIAL
ACCOMPLISHMENT

Many years ago at an entrepreneur conference, I met a man who was responsible for getting people addicted to mobile app games. For decades of his life, he studied the psychology of controlling people's attention. Do you ever notice people staring at their phones aimlessly for 20 minutes straight like they are in a trance? In the same way the bells and whistles of a casino are triggers that release dopamine in your brain, these games are carefully constructed to keep people addicted. More attention in the game means more advertisements shown to the viewers, all resulting in advertising dollars in the pockets of the game companies. They don't care about your goals in life. They want your attention and to keep you addicted. Just like these app games, there are so many False Motivational Traps that make you "feel" motivated and make you "feel" inspired, but in the real world – they get you addicted to good feelings. Negative habits are formed and they keep you running on a hamster wheel. You think you're going somewhere but for months (or years) on end, your life pretty much remains the same. It's not simply enough to "feel" motivated here and there. But that's exactly what motivational traps cause you to do. They are addicting and you'll want to hold onto them because they feel good, similar to a drug addiction. In your mind, you justify this behavior because you're not ready to let it go. Wake. The. Fu*k. Up. These good feelings are often times a trap because you even think you are productive when you are not!

For many hours a day, I would play this numbers puzzle game on my phone. When I beat a level, I told myself that I'm expanding my mind because I'm solving challenging tasks. Zero chapters of my book got written in that timeframe. I gained 5 pounds. And my business hasn't grown. I convinced myself I was being productive when I was simply caught in a trap. Even when I stopped playing that particular game, I moved onto the next thing to feed my rush. Can you see how there is an underlying pattern here regardless of what the surface-level problem is? This doesn't only apply to app games. Even the things you think are helping you also cause you to get caught in the loop.

Please take my advice with a grain of salt and some common sense. I often talk about how people get caught in The Learning Loop. They read lots of books with zero-to-no action. But books are an important part of learning new things. Motivational videos can help you build confidence that you may otherwise lack. But too much of a good thing can lead to an unhealthy addiction. Like everything else, take my words for what they are worth. It's like a see-saw. You may start on one side, then go all the way to the other. But eventually, with the right amount of self-awareness, you balance it off in the middle. Learning and taking action. The ultimate litmus test for this is when you can honestly answer the following question: Am I getting the results I want?

Pay Close Attention to Your Emotions

If I threw you into a large campfire full of snakes, would

you do everything in your power to jump out and escape?

Of course you would.

You see, that's how easy it is to be motivated.

You move away from what feels bad. You move towards what feels good. Not in the future, but right now in the present moment. Think of it as a person with an electrical cord attached to them. When you plug them into the outlet, their body fills with electricity and this is what gets them to move.

Move.

That's a good word. Move. Motion. Putting your body in motion. Logic makes you think but emotions place your body in motion. The secret to motivation is by manipulating your emotions. Which specific emotions actually put your body into motion? For most of us, it's the painful ones. I mean we can dream all day of how great things will feel when we build that million-dollar business, get back in shape, and go out there to do all the things we say we are going to do someday. But we aren't actually doing them today. We are comfortable. And comfort does what? Keeps you in place. Why feel all the pain of exercise when this pizza tastes good now? Look at it this way, if the temperature outside is perfectly warm, will you go running to a shelter? No. But what if it was 50 degrees below zero and ice starts falling from the sky? That is what will get you running!

If it's truly the positive emotions that we are chasing after with our goals, we already have all the positive emotions we need in the present moment. We have them when we feel comfortable and continue on with our bad habits. Yes, the pain comes here and there, but until things get bad enough, it's not enough to push you to move. This leads to us never having a compelling reason to do the things we need to do. Our life ultimately remains the same. More often than not, it's actually the pain that makes you move. In the upcoming pages of this chapter, I'm going to outline a number of things that will make you <u>feel</u> more motivated, but often times they are nothing more than a trap.

Motivational Videos & Inspirational Quotes.

There's this popular motivational video by a man named Eric Thomas who tells a story about a young man wanting to be successful. His mentor says to meet him in the early hours of the morning at the beach. He tells the young man to go into the water. When the young man goes in, he gets instructed to go deeper. All the way until he is far enough where he is underwater and having trouble breathing. The young man struggles to get out of the water and does everything he can to take that much-needed gasp for air. The mentor says "When you want to succeed as much as you want to breathe, that's when you'll be successful."

It's a very powerful motivational video.

I saw this video at least a dozen times when I was trying to get motivated to do things in my life. Just the other day, an intern on my marketing team comes up to me and says he saw this video and it made him feel really motivated. Just like I talked about before, it triggered a flood of dopamine into his brain and this resulted in him to do what? Get more of that reward! 17 motivational videos later, he was still feeling motivated. During that same timeframe, I wrote three chapters of my book and an email for my business.

Here's the problem I have with positive affirmations, motivational videos, and inspirational quotes:

- They make you "feel" motivated.
- They make you "feel" inspired.
- They pump you up with "feel-good" emotions.

But when was the last time you ran a marathon after seeing the latest feel-good inspirational quote on social media?

Never. That's when.

It's one thing to "feel" motivated and to "feel" inspired, but that's not what you're going after, is it? The purpose of motivation is so you are actually doing the things that you need to do, right? One of the main premises I'll talk about later in this book is The Habit Loop where there are three elements:

1. The Trigger Event,
2. The Action, and
3. The Positive Reward.

When a chemical called dopamine gets released into your brain after you do something, this reinforces the action you took to get there. Many actions you're doing feel good but they aren't motivation in the real world for you. This chapter will help you break free from that trap. Or is this chapter a trap in itself? You learn something new so you feel dopamine and you want to read more and more and more. Which is taking you away from what? Doing. That's what.

Mindset, Self-Help, and The Law of Attraction

I might as well give you a heroin needle and strap the rubber band around your arm. This book is about breaking free from an addiction to procrastination and laziness. Not feeling good. There is a fine line between emotional balance, The Law of Attraction, living in "The Now", re-wiring your brain for success, and **motivation**.

One of the things I'd like you to take a look at on your journey right now is the level of work you've been accomplishing in the past few weeks. The past few days for example. Many people read this book after being trapped inside the personal development world for years. They have a positive mindset and are empowered, but they simply aren't accomplishing the goals they visualize for themselves.

So if you're into self-help: Yes, you are going through a phase of your life where you're into personal growth and this is GREAT! Seriously, it is. You've discovered a hidden oasis of information that is seriously changing your life. You're learning how to overcome limiting beliefs, understand the why's and how's of your behaviors, you are empowered to tap into your Limitless potential and you can feel like you can achieve anything in this life. You just know deep down that you're destined to do great things. Pay attention to how you **feel**.

Let me tell you something, it's entirely possible that you will still **feel** that same positivity and self-confidence when you're 95 years old and on your death bed (even if you did nothing with it). It's an emotion inside of you that you feel flowing through your system. Can you see how easy this is to trick you because it feels so real? Self-help serves a positive purpose because in the past you may not have been empowered at all, you were a victim to your circumstances, and you lacked the bullet-proof self-confidence you need to step forward in your life. You installed this new belief system because it broke you free from being a victim of your circumstances. But once again, this is a belief system that should <u>support</u> the motivational actions you take, not replace it. You can know for certain all you want, but unless you let that energy flow from your inner universe to your outer universe, the visions you see for yourself will only be stuck in there, and you'll never experience it out there. This book is about removing that block which clogs up the gap between the two.

What else have you been able to accomplish through personal development and self-growth? You've probably been able to release past emotional baggage and trauma. If you dive deep enough, you started getting more into the spiritual realm. Energy flows, quantum physics, and The Law of Attraction. In the past, you may have had negative thoughts in your mind attract negative experiences into your life. With The Law of Attraction, you experience quick wins, but never long-term sustained lasting results. Right? RIGHT!? But after discovering this, you have a more empowered foundation to work from where you now know you have more control over your thoughts, your emotions, and ultimately crafting your destiny.

The work you're doing in your unconscious mind is like re-writing the hologram of your external reality. In the unconscious mind, these thoughts play a direct role on your behaviors. And because your behaviors lead to your results, if you don't have things figured out in there, it'll be virtually impossible to operate at peak performance levels out there. You learn how to rapidly re-program limiting behaviors and by mastering this inner game of motivation, you've reached a balanced state.

That's what personal development does for you. Unlike 99% of people in the world, you've finally learned how to get shit figured out on the inside. And I'm not being a hater on all of these things. I'm the founder of the personal development company EvolutionLimitless.com that teaches all of these things as well. I've written and published books on emotional balance and happiness. I've also built businesses that have impacted millions of lives with all the stress, struggle, and frustration to get there the first time around (pre-personal development days). It's not an either-or game. It's a mix of both. Inner AND Outer Growth.

Before getting into personal development, I was all about the outer game. I struggled, it was painful, and I had to have strict external accountability groups with punishments for not taking action. I achieved a lot (built the magazine business to 1.3 million readers), but it wasn't unbreakable, long-term, sustained, internal motivation.

After my first business took off, I spent many years of my life focusing 90% of my efforts on the inner game, neglecting my motivation in the real world. On the inside, I was equipped to handle anything physically and emotionally. But on the outside, my levels of success and achievement were suffering. I warn you not from reading this in books, but from my own personal experience of messing things up in my own life itself. Life looks a whole lot different through the lens of running out of money in a foreign country, hiding your car when it's out for repossession, sleeping on couches to get by, and stepping on the scale when you realized that you just put on 50 pounds again.

If self-help is your life, perhaps it's time to start tipping the pendulum back in the other direction. You know, just to balance things out a bit.

Are You Happy with Your Current Habits?

So with that being said, let me challenge you for a second: What have you been doing on the outside? Have you already achieved the results you want? If not, let's ask another question...Are you currently executing on that vision and have already built out the long-term, consistent positive habits that are leading you there? It's ok if you aren't at the end destination yet. If you can look back at the past month and say you've been going to the gym consistently multiple times a week with a good amount of effort there, you're on the right path. As long as you are currently executing on the sustained habits that will continue to move you forward to get there, you've already won in this game of motivation. So that's the ultimate test to see if personal development has worked for you in regards to motivation so far. Are you actually **doing**?

This advice is 100% in relation to motivation.

I want to make a note and I'll repeat it again later. Self-Help is so much more than simply helping you set the stage for motivation. Emotional balance, overcoming fears, boosting confidence, and all these other things can be achieved without being motivated to do other things in life. I love it, I learn more about it, and practice it every week of my life. So I'm not taking away from that and you shouldn't stop. I just know it can be a trap you fall into when you shift your focus to action-taking again. If any of this applies to you, I'd like to give you a boost of confidence and let you know that you're on the right track...

Addictive Patterns & The Learning Loop

You see, one of the fundamental building blocks of human behavior is that we grow accustomed to the patterns that once served us in the past. I once had a client who, when he was 5 years old, got really mad at his parents when he didn't get a treat he wanted. When he asked nicely for the treat, he didn't get it. But when he threw a temper tantrum, they finally caved in; and he got the reward! What happened in this moment in time? A pattern was created that basically states "When I get angry, I get what I want." No matter how destructive this behavior is when it comes to his management style at work and his relationships at home, he can't seem to shake his anger because the pattern is already built. The pattern subconsciously served him at one point in his life and he simply has not found a better alternative yet. The more this behavior served his positive intent over the years, the deeper the groove became carved in the ground. The water continued to flow through it because it was the easiest, most efficient path without any resistance.

The Learning Loop

We grow comfortable and addicted to good feelings so those specific grooves remain there. There's this one YouTube channel I used to follow where the man talks about great personal development topics and I gained a lot of amazing lessons and insights from him. But the problem I noticed (I only noticed this after I broke free) is that I was growing addicted to the new information I was learning and the positive feelings that went along with them. When you learn this new information, you get a dopamine rush to the brain, and these good emotions flood your body as a reward. This reward comes immediately after that behavior and it builds a new habit. But what are you doing when you feel good? What is the habit you're building? Sitting on your ass? Watching another one of their videos? Reading another book? This reward is even stronger when you repeat this information to your friends and you feel the validation when they look up to you for the knowledge you have.

In my first book: I am Not a Millionaire - Making the Shift from Failure to Financial Freedom - I call this The Learning Loop. You learn something new, you feel good, so you repeat the habit and continue to learn, learn, and learn some more; with very little action involved. You practice positive affirmations and have clarity in your goals. But the habit-generating part of your mind is getting rewarded for what? Doing nothing. The YouTuber I used to watch spoke in a hypnotic language with a hypnotic audio file in the background to keep me locked in a trance-like state.

I grew addicted to learning new things in the same way most children get addicted to mindless video games. I "felt" more empowered because I was improving my inner-game, but it took away from serious motivation and productivity in the real world. Months went by and I didn't actually get anything done. You don't have to stop completely but at least start breaking free from the addiction. View this growth as a small side-dish and no longer the main course.

What percentage of your time is in action mode and what percentage of your time is in a mode where you are sitting around "action-faking" as one of my old mentors calls it, doing things that make you feel productive, but are not moving the needle forward towards your goals. Beyond the learning loop, this includes non-important but feel-good tasks. One practical example would be if I spent days twiddling around with the design of the blog on my website instead of doing the most important task of promoting awareness of my books! Can you see the difference in importance between the two?

Zen-Like Feelings

Another important element of motivation is that you should stop dreaming of the long-term goal. Instead, you should shift your focus to the rewards you receive immediately after each positive short-term action. The problem is that many of the actions you should be taking make you feel pain so your emotional body doesn't crave them. When you eat potato chips, it overstimulates your taste buds. The immediate reward is built into the food. When you first transition to eating vegetables, you miss out on this so you don't feel the immediate reward when you eat broccoli. But if you retrain your brain to appreciate the clean energy you get from eating such a raw and natural food, you can find a subtle sense of appreciation from it. Almost a Zen-like state.

I prefer the feelings I get of accomplishment when I reach a new fitness goal or finish a chapter of my book. It's a good feeling to get addicted to. Small wins along the way on a long journey can start letting you know what that feels like. I really can't tell people enough that there is a hidden power in finding a way to love the actions you do in order to get to your destination. When you start to get the same dopamine rush from the positive actions themselves, this is how the positive habits are truly formed.

There's a difference between the clean energy you feel after a healthy meal and being over-stimulated from sugar and salty flavors while eating a junk food snack. When you're addicted to the latter, you may not even know what the Zen-like feeling of flow state feels like. A million times better than the over-stimulating rushes of adrenaline. And a trillion times subtler. It's the difference between mindless cartoons and internet browsing vs. going out and doing sales calls for your business. Learn to appreciate the latter.

Break free of the over-stimulation of motivational videos, pump-up seminars, and inspirational quote memes you share on social media; unless it's truly a thing that gets you to take immediate action afterwards. It's one thing if it actually leads you to action, but for most people it's just another cue to watch the next one.

Social Media

Do you notice the immediate need to check your phone when a new message or notification comes in through text or social media? This stuff is carefully constructed to take your attention away from what you need to be doing and onto the platform that earns money with advertiser dollars for your attention.

Have you found that feeling yet? Tune in a little closer and you'll see it's already there. Sometimes you just have to remove the distractions and the noise.

The Problem with "Just take action!"

Then, there are the YouTube channels and thought leaders who are actually legit with their practical advice. In the business world, I follow Gary Vee and Grant Cardone. Other businessmen at their level (but who don't necessarily have a public appearance) are mentors are mine and preach the hard work, struggle, and pain of growing a business. 14 hour days. Face adversity, failure, and frustration. And they have great practical skills advice. They achieved the results I wanted, so I listen to them!

But many of them scream out "Just do it!" as a way to try to motivate people when there is so much more understanding about human behavior that they are not well-versed in. Human behavior is simple. When we feel good after doing something, we do more of it because we are rewarded by the dopamine receptors that drip chemicals into our brain. When we feel pain after doing something, we do less of it. No matter how much you logically know the deep-dish meat lover's pizza will lead to obesity, diabetes, a stroke, and a heart attack; you keep eating it because you are rewarded for doing what feels good now.

Is "Just do it" good motivational advice? Yes, for the people who listen to it. It takes advanced psychology knowledge to truly fix problems quicker than pushing through it with pain and struggle. There are more advanced things that take away from motivation such as fears of failure and rejection (which I'll talk about in a later chapter). But basically if you want to overcome your fear of failure/rejection with making sales calls, you bring up a picture in your mind, see yourself in the picture as if your worst fear already unfolded. Pay close attention to yourself in the picture and see where the self-judgement is. "I'm a sleazy salesperson who is greedy!" could be what comes to mind for you. When you use an NLP rapid emotional release technique on that picture in your mind, it removes the emotional charge to that fear. With that resistance gone, you open up a portal that allows you to step through and take that action with ease. If you believe selling makes you a sleazy person, you'll resist being a salesperson, even if that's what is needed to achieve your goals. There are two NLP visualization processes that help overcome Limiting Beliefs and open up the portal for taking action.

Logical thinking does not drive human behavior.

Let me repeat that because it's important. Logic. Does. Not. Drive. Human. Behavior. Most practical-advice gurus teach you with logic. You can learn skills and strategies this way and this is a good thing. If you don't know how to do something, learning something new from a mentor is an absolute essential element of moving forward on your journey. But it has very little impact on the bigger scheme of human behavior if you're procrastinating because of a motivational trap.

Pay Attention to Where Your Energy is Flowing

Instead of following the pattern of dopamine and good/bad emotions, I now view motivation through a different lens. For example, imagine that your body is filled with a limitless source of energy. Where is your energy flowing? Is it flowing into something that is building your dream? You plant a seed in the ground with the first action you take on the larger goal of yours. You can choose to transmit this internal energy into those things just like the water that continuously has more and more energy grow the tree over time. Or you can neglect the plant and it would slowly wither away and die. Focus on your goals and pay close attention to where the energy is flowing. My goals lately have been heavily purpose-driven and financially based. When I create a new product and website for my business, I'm building up a money machine that will continue to work for me for a lifetime. When I write my next 12 books this year for you, I'm building a legacy that will help you and the world be more empowered. When it's listed on Amazon and other places, I am building a structure that will last throughout the years.

And then, one day in the future, you will reach the threshold shift. Our bodies are pre-programmed to conserve energy resources. When I expended a lot of energy into my magazine business without getting anything back – my unconscious habits kicked in "Andrew is doing all this work and getting nothing back, this is an energy drain. Stop what you are doing!". Unknowingly, that once I reached the threshold shift, the energy I put into my magazine apps began doing the work for me. I created a self-sustaining machine that produced an endless stream of passive income for me into the many years ahead. It's simply delayed results. They say that a pound of muscle burns 156 calories per day. When you channel your energy into building something, have faith that the threshold shift will balance the forces of nature out, and you'll reap your rewards when you get there.

People in this world are either consumers or producers. When you consume things such as television shows, games, and mindlessly browse social media; these type of things drain and consume your energy. When you get that quick fix, the energy is gone and nothing is produced. But when you unleash your energy out into the world, magical things happen when something gets built. Which direction is your energy flowing?

So move forward on your journey envisioning the seed being planted with the first step you take. And the constant need to water that seed into a plant and eventually into a tree so your energy feeds it and grows it over time.

That's the type of thing you should be going for.

Be careful of feeling a false sense of artificial accomplishment through Dopamine and Motivational Traps.

Chapter 4

Outcome-Based Goal Setting

ALL ARROWS POINTING TO ONE DESTINATION

On March 16, 2012, I packed my clothes and laptop into the back of an old fire-engine red Nissan Sentra and drove 2,000 miles across the country to have lunch with a millionaire I met on the internet. Scottsdale, Arizona was my destination. Down to my last $250, I reached the point in my life where things couldn't get any worse. So why not drive across the country without any clue what I'm doing in hopes for something better? In my mind, this internet millionaire could teach me how to pull myself out of the dreaded financial situation I've been stuck in for all too long. It was a risk, but the worst-case-scenario of failing was suddenly a better option than if I stayed where I was and my life continued to remain the same. The actions I've been doing in the past have led me to where I am today, so it's time to start doing new things if I want to get somewhere else. But just like when I set the clear destination of Scottsdale, when we set goals for ourselves, we always begin with where we want to be going. This is the basis for Outcome-Based Goal Setting. Begin with the end in mind and work your way backwards from there.

What's Your Destination?

Whether it was my childhood goal of being a police officer, being a location-independent entrepreneur who writes books and travels the world, being in great shape again, or having a relationship that is right for me; we all have dreams in life. But how do we motivate ourselves to achieve them? For most of my life, it was spent doing nothing more than dreaming about big goals I never thought I could achieve. I would watch videos of successful people on the internet living the life I wanted to live, reading lots of books, talking about the things I was going to do someday, but each and every time, the problem remained the same.

I wasn't actually doing them.

Many hours after driving across the country and arriving in the desert of Scottsdale, late into the night, my lucky break finally came. I bet the last $250 I had on a game of poker and earned just under $2,000 to help begin a new chapter of turning my life around in my new home of Arizona. I reached my first destination, but what am I going to do next?

Playing to Win vs. Playing to 'Not Lose'

Most of my life was spent playing to Not Lose, which is light years away from playing to win. It wasn't until a few weeks later before I fully understood what this meant for motivation and achieving our goals. I used to always focus on the bad things that were going wrong in my life, the reasons why something couldn't be done, excuses that got in the way, the infamous "What if...", and avoiding the things I didn't want to happen. The comfort zone of my miserable situation was chosen over the perceived pain of failure and rejection every single time. But what if none of that matters if you are truly committed to going after what you want?

Sometimes we have to look at this from a different perspective to see how this holds true in our lives. I was at an outdoor nightclub called American Junkie with my roommate AJ at the time. The nightlife of Scottsdale, Arizona is a hidden gem in the middle of the desert. Both of us just took the leap of faith and moved to Arizona from the East Coast. Going out here tonight was the perfect way to build out our social lives.

Upon arriving that night, there was this one man named Leon instructing a group of five younger guys how to meet girls at a bar. In the men's dating advice community, they call these boot camps. Young guys would pay experienced instructors and coaches $2,000 - $3,000 for the weekend teaching them how to meet and attract women. One of the students there had Leon standing over him, both hands on his shoulders, saying in the boy's ear, "Go talk to the one in the red".

A group of 5 or 6 very attractive women, one wearing a red dress that drew the attention of men from miles away, was surrounded by a group of strong-looking well-dressed attractive men. Any young man trying to build up his confidence would be slightly intimidated (at best). Paralyzed by fear, at worst.

Not knowing what to say or how they would react, he built up stories in his mind of getting rejected, judged, and perhaps in a physical altercation if she has a boyfriend in the group. The worst-case outcome always plays through our minds as a survival mechanism to keep us alive. His body grew tense, he froze up where he was, and he wouldn't budge. Eventually, Leon got him off-balance, pushed the guy in the middle of the group, he got embarrassed, apologized, and quickly scurried away to the other side of the bar.

"The problem with most people is that they are actually not playing to win. They are playing to not lose", I overheard Leon saying to his students. Was the student's goal to talk to the girl or simply to not get rejected? When he set the goal in his mind to not get rejected, he unconsciously moved towards it. On the outside, he says he wants one thing (to improve his dating life), but in his behaviors, it's a different story.

Whether it's with dating, business and sales, or fearing the embarrassment and shame of going to the gym when you're overweight; if we spend our time moving away from what we don't want, we aren't necessarily moving towards what we do want in life. While there is an emotional aspect to these fears, it all starts with the mental focus of pointing all arrows towards one singular destination.

It's like going on a road trip to the other side of the country without knowing exactly where you want to arrive. You might want to escape your small town in Alabama but if you just get up and drive, you'll be going around in circles not having the proper direction and focus to get to where you want to be. Someone packing up their life and moving to Hollywood to chase their dreams of being a famous actor one day is a better example of someone with a more Well-Defined Destination. If you imagine a person playing archery with a red bullseye in the middle of the target, this is the way to channel your motivation in the right direction by keeping your eye on the prize.

Setting Your Destination

The most important thing to always do first is to set a clear destination to work towards. This is the outcome you want to be achieving after your work is done. Most people who struggle with a lack of motivation don't have a clearly-defined purpose or outcome they are moving towards. Can you see that by having a very clear outcome or goal that you want to achieve, this can provide you with the focus and direction to at least start getting in the right direction? Many of us dreamers in life know what we want, but may simply lack the motivation to start going there. That's what this book will help you with. Other people might not know what they want and are too busy thinking about how fat, poor, and lonely they are. I used to be like that and all it did was keep me in a depressive thought loop pattern for years. So it all starts with understanding the exact destination first before you put the boots on and start marching that way!

I know what mine is. In my book Define Your Purpose: Meaning, Fulfillment, and Direction in Life, I talk about how I can't put words to it, but it's this gravitational force that is stronger than a black hole. No matter what I do in life, it's just something that pulls me in. It's just a deeply-rooted feeling.

In 2016, I joined one of the largest growing social justice movements of the 21st century; The Animal Rights Movement. In this community of motivated individuals, I often found them spending their days, nights, and even weekends motivated to move towards their purpose. Often times, at great personal risk and sacrifice to themselves.

What moves them?

According to the vegan lifestyle, all living beings deserve life and we should not be eating animals for food. There is an abundant amount of food made up of fruits, nuts, grains, vegetables. Plenty of plant-based doctors created diet plans to meet all of our nutritional requirements to support life. But at the core of it, this lifestyle is not so much about diet, but the moral obligation to save the lives of animals. Whether you share in this philosophy or not, you can surely appreciate how this entire movement of millions of people are all working towards one clearly-defined goal. Saving the lives of animals in any way possible. "Until all animals are free" is the quote one small group of activists live by.

But what if you don't know the exact steps it takes to get there? Well, that's something we'll talk about in the next chapter because they could choose a million things that lead them to their goal. In the **Why, What, How Formula**; this is What you do. I want to build a location-independent business that allows me to work from anywhere in the world and provides me passive income from the work I've done. I want to be 180 pounds with muscle and a low body fat percentage. I want to be in the relationship of my dreams. This is What I want in my life. I know Why I want it. So the How could be writing books, by inventing a product and selling it on a website, investing in stocks, or a million other things.

In the Colorado Rocky Mountains, there are 48 mountains with peaks above 14,000 feet. People make it a goal to climb many of them. Can you see how you must first choose which peak you want to reach before you can choose the path (How) to get there?

Even for the Billionaire entrepreneur Elon Musk who set his destination of colonizing Mars and turning humans into an interplanetary species, he has that vision of a colony on Mars first. In stage 1 of his plan, he is currently the founder of a company called SpaceX, which makes billions of dollars building larger rocket ships than NASA and companies pay him $20 million a pop to launch their satellites into space. Small steps in the right direction, but can you see how it all starts with his goal of the colony on Mars? On the flip side, what if he invented a new type of rocket propulsion system similar to the ones you see in space movies? That can be one step to help get him there too.

- First, you have your Why.
- Then, you have your What.
- In the next chapter, we can move to How.

What's The End Goal for You?

So, as long as you have the understanding that there can be many pathways towards your clearly-defined vision and goal; it all starts with this destination in mind. Can you see with the example of the guy avoiding rejection and not even talking to the girl – he moved towards the goal he set for himself (not getting rejected) but away from what he actually wanted? The aspiring actor moving to Hollywood knows where they are going on the first leg of their journey. And every morning, I'm moving towards the positive vision of what I want with my books and impact on the world. To help me keep clear and focused, I make a lot of conscious effort to choose my end destination and write it down on a piece of paper. This way, I can maintain the clear focus and re-alignment when I feel like I may be going off course, jumping to a new idea when I face adversity or setback, or lose focus of what's important to me.

Creating the Right Mental Programming

There is a mechanism in your brain called the Reticular Activating System (RAS) which is your selective focus. Imagine that you're at a movie theater.

1. **The Movie on the Screen –** This is the result of your perception and awareness. It's what you notice in the world.
2. **The Movie Reel –** This is where you choose to focus your attention and awareness.
3. **The White Light of the Projector –** This is what shines through the filters in your mind.

Similar to the slides you put in a movie reel at a movie theater, the RAS can't process a negative. Just like the young man at the nightclub in Scottsdale, his awareness was on "not getting rejected", so his mental perception projects into the world "getting rejected" because his RAS cuts off the "not". His perception saw all the reasons why he would get rejected. But if he shifted his awareness to having a great conversation with someone new, he would automatically begin noticing things that would align with that. The world is full of meaningless energy,and we project our perception onto the world based on this psychological trait. But in addition to that, when that's where his focus is, he will also be subconsciously programming his behaviors to align with "getting rejected" because his mind can't hear the Not.

What if he simply removed that slide and set the new intent? He could be focusing on building up the confidence to push through his fear of talking to strangers. What if the rookie salesperson focused his efforts on making sales calls, going after the sale, instead of avoiding rejection and never picking up the phone?

There is No Failure, Only Learning

What if in both instances they have the understanding that they will face 100 failures before their first success? That when you focus on gaining the experience and building the skills (even if you don't succeed with your goal right away), it's a better option than moving away from what you don't want? Even the best baseball player in the world has to strike out countless amounts of times before he gets his first homerun. The only difference for him is that he understands that striking out from time to time is a normal part of the process. And you should too.

Out of the 2,000,000 bits of information that bombard your senses at every given moment, your mind only consciously takes in 150 of those bits. This means you are only aware of 0.000075% of what's actually happening around you right now. The more you build your RAS to focus on what you do want, the more it trains your awareness to automatically and effortlessly bring things into your awareness that move you towards that. Maybe you overhear a conversation one day that you might have otherwise missed. The people next to you talk about the free month membership at a local gym you can go to. Or you see an advertisement for a position in another company that pays more money than what you're currently making. I can't put in words enough how focusing on what you do want is one of the most important things you can do at this stage of your journey for setting your goals. Have you ever tried to climb a mountain or run a marathon through the city streets while only looking behind you? Not a good idea…

Remove the Excuses

A lot of people have a chronic habit of focusing on all the things wrong in their lives, all the reasons why things can't be done, all the fears that hold them back, and all the excuses that are not aligned with achieving. Their 0.000075% of information has been flooding their entire awareness for so long, they can't even break free and see the 99.9925% of what they could start focusing on right now. It takes a decision to break free of a victim, problem-focused, fear-fueled, rear-view-mirror facing mindset; and to focus on looking forward at the things in your life that can make it happen. Yes, obstacles are there. But when you start searching for the solution, you'll find that there too. Once you train your brain to focus on the empowering positive future towards a clear goal; it does wonders for aligning your focus from there.

Be as Specific as Possible – The How

In the next chapter of this book, we'll drill down in the details on finding the pathway to take and really understand how you will get there. But for now, let's start carving the general pathway with the specifics that will lead you to your goal. It pays to be specific. Many times we set general goals for ourselves such as making more money or losing more weight. This makes it difficult to narrow our focus even further in order to uncover the pathway to get there. An example with fitness would be if a person sets a vague goal of wanting to get in better shape.

- Do they want to slim down by eating less calories?
- Do they want to lose 20 pounds with the same diet but heavy on exercise?
- Do they want to speed up to run a marathon?
- Or do they want to bulk up and lift really heavy weights?

If a person trains for a marathon one day, slims down for three weeks, and then decides they want to be a heavy bodybuilder a week after that, they would be all over the place. That would be like zig zagging from left to right back to left again instead of setting a clear line to their destination.

All Great Things Take Time to Build

Do you ever notice that when a person goes to the gym for a week, you don't see a change in their appearance right away? But when you look at a person who started going to the gym today and remained consistent with their goal for 3 months straight, you'll see the noticeable difference over time. Right? Why do you expect anything different for yourself? A steady progression of consistent energy into one thing is important.

Just like building a sandcastle at a beach, you can't put one bucket of sand down, the second, and the third expecting the project to be completed right away. Only to get discouraged, give up and start from scratch 10 feet further down the beach. Stick with one core goal and the more buckets of sand you put down, the more energy you are putting towards building that one very specific thing. Many people who try to achieve big things have a false expectation of seeing results right away. Putting up a website and making thousands of dollars overnight. Losing 15 pounds in the next 7 days. Finding and maintaining the relationship of their dreams overnight without all the nuances it takes to build something great over time. Building out the full vision takes time and patience is a virtue that unfortunately many people don't appreciate.

Why. What. How.

The animal rights activists seeking to set every animal free is not something that they put a little bit of effort into and give up on. They know What they want. They choose the right path How to get there. And their Why is the glue that keeps them going until completion. The salesperson doesn't make 10 cold calls and becomes a pro at closing the deal. So can you see how important it is to have one clear destination, the right Why to keep you to it, and to expect a long-term consistent path to get there? Can you also understand how destructive it is to shift all of your energy into something else when your false expectations are not met right away? Patience is a virtue. Use it.

One of the main biological traits of human behavior is that the unconscious mind always seeks the path of least resistance. Back in the caveman days, do you go on the trail covered in poisonous snakes and 10 miles into the distance to get water? Or do you go to the waterfall that is 20 feet away and safe? We are always looking for that immediate gratification, so that's why it's important to build up your Why and your focus towards one specific destination so you can utilize this knowledge to align with the right track. The people you see having success doing something else went on their own long-term journey behind the scenes of the success you see on the outside. They faced the adversity and setbacks you faced, but they pushed through it. Don't jump ship when you face the first sign of resistance.

You Can Only Walk One Trail at a Time

But what if you can get even more specific with your goals? Just like the goal of the animal rights and vegan community is to set all animals free, my very specific piece of the vision I'm putting my energy into is building out the vegan food business that helps people take the first small steps in the right direction. I've been to other types of activism events, but with the limited amount of time and energy we have in this life, we can't do everything. We are one year into the business since I started and we are nowhere near the millions of people eating our meals that we are shooting for. But we've made significant progress that is finally showing results on the outside come to fruition.

Clear vs. Vague

When I compare this clear vision of "Easy Pre-Cooked Vegan Meals" to my business goals 10 years ago of simply making money online and quitting my job, I wasn't specific enough as to where I was putting my actions and energy into. Because my goal was to make money, I would jump from idea to idea when I didn't see results right away. I thought I could make money with affiliate marketing. So I tried that for a few weeks, and then I stopped. I switched to selling online courses for a month or two. I made a few sales, and then when my friend started selling pet products to the tune of $45,000 per month, I stopped and tried that too. I was chasing the money, which could come from a million different directions.

When I finally committed to building a portfolio of 20 different digital magazine apps for six months, regardless of any failures that I faced (I faced hundreds of them), the work I put into this eventually allowed me to build a digital publishing company up to 1.3 million readers. I would have never had this success if I wasn't very specific with the What and How I was doing it, fueled by my Why.

Re-Focus This Advice on Your Goals

How narrow is your focus with your goal? Do you want to lose weight? Or do you want to gain 20 pounds of muscle by lifting weights at the gym 3 times a week? Do you want to make money through a business, or do you want to write a book that helps people become more motivated in their lives? In the game of patience and persistence, clearly-defined specific goals win every single time. Be specific with the goals you set out for yourself. And know what you're putting your energy into because that will build up when you put it into one thing. **What's your destination?** How many buckets of sand have you put down?

Before you set your goal in stone, there are a lot of different factors you should take into consideration to make sure you want it. Your Why is one of them. But there are others as well.

What Do You Stand to Lose by Achieving It?

The day I quit my job and became a location-independent entrepreneur who made money in my sleep was a great financial success for me. I left the job I hated, packed up my car in the scotching hot Scottsdale, Arizona summer and drove up to the mountains towards the cool Boulder, Colorado landscape. All my dreams have come true, but there were many sacrifices in the process. When I spent 100% of my free time building my business, I neglected going to the gym. I completely gave up. I was heavier than I could ever imagine in my life. My lack of meaningful connections and social life was directly connected to plugging away at my computer all the time building my magazine business.

A couple years later, my third time of moving to Boulder, Colorado while traveling, I lost 50 pounds in the matter of three months by hiking the most challenging mountain in the city every morning. I was out of energy by mid-day and it took a toll on my energy levels to put into my business. But my fitness goals were reached.

So the important thing to really think about when you set goals for yourself is how they impact other areas of your life. In some instances, they could positively impact them. Building my second business years later freed up my time to get in shape by exercising and climbing mountains every morning. But in many instances, it can negatively impact other areas of your life (and happiness) too. I know many businessmen and woman who become workaholics and this leads to unhappiness, stress, divorce, and health problems in their personal life.

Think about what's important to you in your life, make a list of all the top areas and try to work out a schedule to fit it all in. While many of the greatest achievers in this world preach making sacrifices in order to achieve their goals (this is 100% right), I suggest putting at least 10% effort into areas of your life that you might be neglecting as well.

Turning Your Goals into a Vision that Comes Alive

It's one thing to logically say what you want. To place some words on a two-dimensional piece of paper. But one way the unconscious mind programs the RAS to spot new opportunities is when you create a clear three-dimensional vision in your mind to make these goals come alive. Close your eyes and imagine that you're already living your goal right now.

What would life be like when you already achieved your goal? What would you be seeing if you had already achieved this goal right now? What would you be hearing? What would it feel like if you already achieved your goal right now? Take a few minutes to close your eyes and visualize/feel like you already achieved it. Adjust the brightness, clarity, and feelings in your body as if you already achieved it right now.

From this visualization standpoint, look into the future and think about what will you do next now that you already have it? After all, this goal is one small stepping stone on a larger journey in life. Do you see yourself continuing to do the things you are doing here because they are joyful to you?

Or is it something else? Also, look back in time and notice the steps you took in order to get to where you are today. These visualization techniques help provide clarity and a new perspective. It helps turn your vague idea of a goal into a more clearly-defined vision that you can hold true for the long-term. If you don't have your vision yet, it's fine. Perhaps, it might be better at this point if you don't have it set in stone yet. In Define Your Purpose: Meaning, Fulfillment, and Direction in Life, I talk about a lot of things to narrow this down.

Never Settle for Less – Be Unreasonable

Often times, we don't go after a goal because we think it's too big for us. We haven't done anything like this before and it might lead us to doubting our abilities if we could ever accomplish it. If you don't think you can achieve the bigger vision, you will set the bar lower for yourself, and look back saying "Now that I actually achieved THIS goal, I should have shot a little bit higher". When I set the goal of $10,000 per month in passive income with my first business, I achieved it. My roommate set a goal of $45,000 per month in the same timeframe. He achieved it. When you set a goal for yourself, your mind finds opportunities that are aligned with getting there with equal amount of work and equal amount of time. Imagine the difference of one person begging investors for $10,000 each to raise $1 million for his business, or going to one Venture Capital firm and asking for $1 million. Same time involved. But the mindset he comes from is different than the other. The first one would have to get 100 people to say yes, while all it takes is one VC firm to agree to it.

Don't let other people convince you that you're being crazy or unrealistic. No great person in this world who accomplished breakthrough things did something that was already done before. All of them surely faced The Outside Critics. People who try to hold them back from success and list all of the reasons why they shouldn't even try.

But it's that Inner Critic that often holds us back from

even trying. That's when you don't believe in yourself. After coaching hundreds of people one-on-one, I've seen people from all starting points and all walks of life accomplish the impossible and achieve great things that were once outside their scope of reality. Doubt kills more dreams than failure ever will. Your past experiences and current situations do not dictate who you are and what you're capable of. Aim a little bit higher. It's one thing for me to say that most people set goals too low for themselves, but it's another thing to experience it for yourself.

When setting you vision for the future, think a little bit bigger, and don't settle for anything less than what would truly make you happy. Trust me on it. Aim for the stars and with the right level of motivation, persistence, and effort; you can get there. And even if you hit 75% of your goal, it's a better option than aiming too low and achieving it.

So if you're not fully clear with your vision just yet, that's fine. The upcoming sections of this book will help you remove the doubt and limiting beliefs that hold you back from setting the true destination you want to be at. They will help you mitigate your fears and your risks so you can step forward into the darkness with confidence. They will provide you with the organizational methods to prevent overwhelm. The clarity to give you focus and direction, and the access to new skills, tools, and resources that have previously never been there for you.

Conclusion

But when we wrap this chapter up, I want to leave you with the reasonable expectation that you will face failures and setbacks along the way. Just like going on a road trip, there is one specific destination that you are working towards. The pin-pointed location on the map. That no matter what you do, you might need to take detours, there might be traffic jams that slow you down, flat tires and broken-down engines that make you feel like giving up, and setbacks that take you 100 miles off course, making you think you're moving backwards when one day you'll learn it's a new direction you actually had to follow, you might need to take a different method of transportation to get there. Trust me when I say this – All great things in life like these goals take time. Set ONE specific destination that is aligned with your WHY and stick with it. But first – you have to know exactly where THERE is.

And most importantly, when you get there; make sure it's actually a place you want to be. The initial rush of achieving your goals will feel good, but then that'll be your new normal and you may wind up feeling the same as you do now. You'll set another goal for yourself, and when you achieve that, you'll set another. It'll be a continuous journey to new and greater things in life. So take an understanding that this goal you set out for yourself is one stepping stone on a larger journey in life. If the thing you're doing is meaningful enough to you, you can actually enjoy every step of the way, no matter how crazy that sounds right now.

In the next chapter, you'll learn how to find the step-by-step path to get there, reduce overwhelm, and know exactly what the one thing you need to be focused on is.

Chapter 5

The Step-by-Step Path

HOW TO ELIMINATE OVERWHELM AND KNOW EXACTLY WHAT STEPS TO TAKE

Many people know what their destination is but they simply don't have the exact steps they need to take in order to get there. They might have zero clue what they're doing, they only have a vague sense of direction, or they're overwhelmed by all the different possibilities and options of things they can do; unable to select one to start with. On the other hand, some people only know the first few steps they can take right now without the confidence and certainty of it leading them in the right direction towards their end goal. They fear they are wasting their time. They do a few things, they don't see any noticeable results right away, and this leads them to give up at the first sign of adversity. Their mind fills up with so many thoughts of what needs to get done and new ideas of all the different things they could be doing instead. This pulls them in a million different directions, which leaves them feeling overwhelmed and stuck in place by analysis paralysis. What happens as a result of this? They're not doing anything!

Instead, imagine what it would be like if you had a step-by-step path clearly outlined for you, a map, and a plan that gives you the confidence of guaranteed success when you do these things. You know exactly what the next step is. You know exactly how to learn new skills for things you've never done before. You have the certainty that you're on the right track and the self-confidence that you have what it takes. Perfectly capable of achieving this new goal for yourself. With this clear start-to-finish outline, all you have to do is move forward and you're destined for success. So how do we get there?

Narrow Your Focus & Avoid Temptations

I finished the last chapter by having you narrow down your focus into one specific way to achieve your goal. There are many trails that lead to the top of the mountain, but you can only walk one of them at a time. For my desire to be a location-independent entrepreneur who earns passive income while I travel the world, I chose the pathway of creating Digital Magazine Apps. It is within this pathway that I narrowed my focus and applied the principles you are going to learn in this chapter to get started with taking action. I began hiking this single trail, and after 8 months, I finally got my results and I achieved my goal! No matter how much failure and adversity I would face on this path, I stuck clear to this one specific destination and never gave along the way. While the tactics, strategies, and actions I take along the way change based on the feedback I get, my vision is timeless and will forever remain the same. Where most people give up, this is where you stay focused. Keep all arrows pointing towards one very clear, specific destination.

Finding the Path to an Undiscovered Magical Land

When we set large goals for ourselves, it's not like you know where the location is on a map. If I want to go to Disney World, it's obvious that I'll plotting my course for Florida. When Elon Musk sets a vision to make humans an inter-planetary species by colonizing Mars, that's the equivalent to some mythical fairytale land in the middle of Narnia. How do we get there? Does the trail even exist? Or do I have to go out there into the unknown and blaze it myself? Utilizing this formula, we'll take your Destination and then start plotting the course to get there; working backwards from the end goal and moving it down the mountain all the way to the starting point. This is a whole different strategy as opposed to blinding staring up into the darkness before your first step. Not only does this light up a clear pathway that leads to your goal, but you'll also clearly see the steps from start to finish. The end result? You'll be provided with the confidence and certainty you need in order to be committed to taking the first step.

Elon Musk started a company called SpaceX which makes billions of dollars launching satellites into space. Through this company, he created new types of rocket ships that are reusable and larger in size than ever before. This one small goal on the way to his larger vision has a company that currently transports satellites into space. But, at the same time, it is also paving the way for reaching Mars with the supplies and resources required to survive there. Can you see how within each larger goal is another sub-goal in itself? No matter how large or small your goal may be, the process is the same. For Elon, he began with the big goal, and then took it down a notch to the space transportation company. When he breaks that down even further, he has the design of the rocket ship. You can break this goal all the way down to buying the metal and supplies that are used to build the rocket.

The Way Our Brain Stores Information

In order to create an effective pathway, you need to know how your brain organizes and stores information. This prevents you from being confused and overwhelmed by disorganized thoughts. In this chapter you're going to learn the psychological structure for how your brain stores information. Imagine if you walk into an office and the files and papers are scattered all over the floor. There will be so much to do, you won't know where to get started. This is the psychological equivalent of having everything organized in alphabetical order in a filing cabinet.

In my Neuro-Linguistic Programming (NLP) training, we call this The Hierarchy of Ideas. Think of this as viewing something from the bigger picture task (I have to get in shape, I have to do the thesis for my degree program, I have to write a book, I have to build a business) and then breaking it down into its individual components. This allows you go from bigger picture (overwhelm) all the way down to one very specific step (focus). If you're stuck in overwhelm, you'll never focus on doing the things you need to do. If you are stuck in laser-focus mode, you won't be able to connect the dots to the bigger picture to make sure you're on the right track. The ability to easily and effortlessly navigate through this structure and these levels is an important part of your success. The mission for this chapter is to take your larger goal and break it down into the one individual step you can take right now.

The Now Step:

- I have to put on my running shoes,
- I have to call my thesis advisor for advice,
- I have to open up Microsoft Word and write the title of the book, etc.
- I have to buy a domain name for my business.

Let's begin with the top level and work our way down from there...

The Bigger Picture (Chunked Up)

Imagine for a moment that the world is in an environmental crisis and you're looking at it from space. The drilling into the Earth's deeper layers for oil takes away the lubricant so the tectonic plates no longer shift as smoothly as they should. There are more earthquakes and more natural disasters due to this imbalance. You can see this from high above, as there are drilling stations positioned all across the globe. But this type of intelligence is way out of sight from the human eye on the surface. From this perspective, you are inspired to make a change, but you're too far up in the bigger picture to do anything about it. You're in planning mode and you're left feeling overwhelmed with so many things to do.

The Smaller Picture (Chunked Down)

Meet Bob. Bob works on an oil rig off of the coast of New Orleans, Louisiana. He mans the machinery in the rig that pushes the drill further and further into the ground with the sole intention to strike oil. He knows how to drill the oil, send it off for processing, and his job is done. From his perspective, he is motivated to do the work and he's getting things done; but he can't see the bigger picture. He has managers above him in the company that sends the oil away on a ship. Higher-level leaders in the company connect the ship's route to the processing facility and connect that processing facility to distribute the gasoline to gas stations across the globe.

People like Bob are motivated and are taking action. But they also have a clear organizational structure above them to make sure they're on the right track and the system functions as a whole. The problem with people in Bob's position is that they are not accessing the levels that are required for self-motivation and self-direction in life; such as starting their own business or finding the right diet and exercise plan for them. Can you clearly see how there is the planning view from space, high-level and mid-level chunks similar to the manager's positions, and then the action steps Bob takes on the ground? Your job is to master the ability to rapidly shift between all levels of the Hierarchy of Ideas and never get caught in one for too long.

The Parallels (Lateral Chunk)

While Bob is working an Oil Rig off the coast of New Orleans, there are other people drilling for oil (at his same level) in the deserts of Saudi Arabia. There are other members of his organization working at oil refineries miles away from The Port of New Jersey, gas station attendants in South America, and millions of people worldwide who are laterally contributing to this bigger vision. A lateral chunk is a different task at the same level. Because they are working in different parts of the system, there is no communication between the parts, as they are not working together. In fact, there are hundreds of other companies and thousands of different drilling sites across the globe where people are not seeing how their actions are connecting together and contributing to The Bigger Picture vision of seeing the Earth from space. While you can chunk up and down to different layers, the lateral chunk is moving between tasks at the same level.

For my book, one action step is to write this specific chapter and a lateral chunk is to write another chapter on setting your destination. Chunking up would be the bigger goal for completing all the chapters together. A lateral chunk from the "complete chapters" goal would be the category of having the book cover design completed. Chunking down within the book cover design category, there would be the Now Step of choosing the background color for the book cover in Photoshop.

Can you clearly see how the Chunked Up vision can see a lot of the moving parts, while the chunked down pieces are the ones doing the small action-steps, but without the bigger vision or lateral communication, the chunked down pieces can't see how it's all tying together?

So how does this apply to you and your motivation?

When you are able to look at things from The Bigger Picture perspective, you can have a clearer understanding of what tasks you should be doing. When you figure out what tasks you should be doing, this can allow you to uncover the resources to help you learn how to do them. When you see all the tasks that lead up to the bigger goal, you can confidently say to yourself, "When I accomplish all of these tasks, I will reach my goal."

When you remove yourself from the Space Station, your boots can hit the ground and you can Chunk all the way down to the Now Step. This gets you to do the one thing you should be doing so you can be one step closer to your destination.

- Are you able to chunk up to gain organization?

- Can you chunk all the way down to focus on one step for action mode?
- Can you chunk laterally to have clear communication between all the parts?

Once you master all three areas, you'll have the confidence you're stepping in the right direction and a clear plan of action to go from there. This will lead you to the next chapters of this book which go into motivation strategies to actually get your body in motion.

What's your Now Step?

A Practical Example - Writing This Book

When I follow my formula for Deconstructing Motivation, I start with the end in mind. Complete paperback and digital copies of the book that help people become more motivated to work towards their goals in life. From the Chunked Up perspective, the book needs to be completed. I'm sure you can visualize the final Destination of the book because you're reading it right now. You're at the top floor of the Skyscraper.

To start finding the path to get there, let's chunk it down a notch by going one level below that. I would ask myself in the general sense, what would have to be done in order to have the book be complete?

- I will need X amount of **chapters written**.
- I will need the chapters **edited**.
- I will need the **book cover designed**.
- I will need to format the book to **publish**.

As you can see, these tasks are chunked one level down from the bigger vision. Each one of these tasks is a lateral chunk of one another (a different piece of the puzzle). But you can chunk down even more below each level.

Underneath each mid-level task are specific tasks that make up that one element. So let's choose one. In order for the book cover to be complete, I need to break that down into its individual elements, and make this into a checklist of things to do.

The book cover needs:

- A proper-sized Photoshop template.
- The background image/color.
- The title of the book.
- The subtitle of the book.
- The author name.
- The barcode on the back.
- The description on the back.
- The information on the spine of the book, and
- Finally - it needs to be edited, approved, and uploaded to the printing company's systems to be able to print.

Each and every one of these tasks is part of a checklist. When every one of these items are checked, then this Book Cover task is marked complete. I can chunk back up from my Now Step, move laterally, and repeat the process for all the higher-level lateral chunks (writing, website, editing, publishing).

Can you see now that regardless of the content of what you're working towards, this structure is the same? I follow the same process for building my business, writing the lyrics for a music album, as well as other things in my life. This organization is a key element to remove overwhelm and know what steps need to be taken in order to get things done. But most importantly, it allows you to arrive at The Now step with the confidence that it's the right thing you need to do first. When you have this, you can channel all of your focus and energy into this one thing until it is complete and gets done. Rinse & Repeat.

Warning: Don't Get Stuck in Planning Mode

On a very important note, you're never going to have the exact plan perfect in the beginning. Many people try to plan everything, they strive for perfectionism, not realizing that there is a whole dynamic system of adjustments along the way. You can spend two months drawing up the perfect business plan, only to find out that after the first step you take, it goes out the window. In the advertising community, we were taught about optimizing and adjusting every step of the way. We create an advertisement with the same words, but five different pictures. When 10,000 people see each of the five variations, we find out which picture gets the most clicks, and then move forward with that one. Things like this are not something you can know for certain up front, so there is a level of stepping forward into the darkness, having faith that you're on the right path, that you might step off course a few times along the way; and not get caught in a planning loop for all too long.

I live with a belief system that in a higher dimensional realm, the future goal you set out for yourself is already here. When you take the next step, the following one will unfold itself as if the universe is lining up to reward you on your path. You won't be handed every gift all at once. When the student is ready, the mentor appears. It's this type of belief system that allows us to stand on the edge of darkness and jump into the light. So rest assured that you won't get things 100% correct in your planning stage. When outlining all the chapters of my book I thought of three great new topics that had to be included, so this organizational system allows me to go back and edit from there. So find the right balance of planning and action, going back and forth along the way. Don't plan for too long.

The Pathway is Organized

So why is this effective? Your unconscious mind processes all of this information at the same time anyway. This is simply a way of organizing it for you so you're no longer overwhelmed. The pathway is created. When you execute on these checklists of high, medium, and low-level tasks, you're confident that the road is there to get you to where you want to be going. If you're new to this thinking, that's great - because you're now going through the natural learning curve that everybody goes through to get better at this over time. A constant outside reminder such as a mentor or a coach could help you build these habits faster than if you do it yourself.

One Final Example – Losing Weight

You can apply this format to a goal of cutting down on body fat, increasing muscle mass, and getting in better shape. That's the destination. Chunking it down a level you can break it into two categories of exercise and diet. Breaking down your diet into its individual components would be to research a proper diet plan used by people who already accomplished your goals, and perhaps hiring a nutritionist who has the experience to do it for you. You arrive all the way down to the now step of picking up the apple you eat for breakfast.

Then, chunk back up to the (diet + exercise) level, and laterally to the exercise side of things. You can work with a personal trainer to get a plan in place that meets your needs. Or do your research online for the workout plan. Break that workout plan down into a daily checklist. Your now step could be to jog one mile on a treadmill tonight. At the end of your workout after you get home, chunk back up to see the list of the week and plan your next day. Can you see how easy this is to get done?

The shortcut to getting to where you want to go faster is to work with people who already have the expertise and skills you don't. As long as the different pieces of the puzzle are put together, you don't always have to be the one to get that piece done. This is where a worker turns into a manager. While I often times open up Adobe Photoshop to make changes to my book covers, the bulk of the work comes from the graphic designer for my publishing company, Derek. He checks the marks on those items and I am hiring an editor who will do the same.

Chunking Up - Allows you to get into planning mode. It's like the man in the space station who sees a ship on the ocean from high up above, able to tell the ship that they are on the right course.

Chunking Laterally - Allows you to connect the pieces together and realize that there are many pathways and many branches to get there. Allows you to plan enough to get the full thing connected. The path is created

Chunking Down - This takes you out of planning mode, removes overwhelm, and when you chunk down to the very first step, The Now Step, this places you in action mode.

What's your Now Step?

Don't simply choose a task that will make you feel good. What's the most important thing that will do the best job of moving the needle forward right now? Just like for me, it could be downloading the book cover Photoshop template, opening up Microsoft Word and putting the title in the book, someone doing a Google search for a Nutritionist, or putting on their running shoes and walking out the front door - there are many different steps you can choose from, so just choose one because the rest will come later.

Otherwise you'll get stuck in analysis paralysis mode forever and your life will continue to remain the same.

What's Your Now Step?

_____

Chapter 6

Motivational Drivers

BIOLOGICAL DRIVERS OF HUMAN BEHVAVIOR
PROGRAMMED TO GET YOU IN MOTION

In the earlier chapters of this book, I talked about how there is a deeper structure of human behavior. When you understand this algorithm of human programming; you know exactly how the body is pre-programmed to behave. Most people go against this programming to try to motivate themselves to do things they don't want to do. They give up. But instead, the solution is to work within your existing biological drivers of behavior. When you begin to understand how your body is naturally programmed to behave, motivation becomes virtually effortless.

The Four Steps You've Taken So Far:
1. Clearly define the destination you want to work towards.
2. Work your way back from the end goal, outlining the major steps you need to take,
3. Get more specific and create a checklist of each thing you need to do for each major task, and
4. Find the one specific action you can take right now and put all of your focus and attention into that one thing. That one thing is called your Now Step.

Now, you're standing at the entrance of a long dark tunnel with this small glimmer of light shining through from the other side. You hope your goal is there so you want to be motivated to take those next steps forward. For many people, they never take those first steps for a lot of reasons. They doubt that they are even going to achieve it. This is especially true for big goals they've never achieved before. They have fears of all the uncertainty within the darkness of the tunnel. There are so many things that act as a force field that prevents them from running forward through the tunnel to their destination on the other side. You may also doubt that the destination is even there. You're standing in your tracks.

What's it going to take to move?

That's the big question. What specifically will it take in order for you to get your body in motion? As I mentioned many times before in this book, the motivation is going to be fueled by the immediate pain. Similar to a caveman who puts his hand in a campfire, he is going to instinctually pull it out as quickly as possible. No motivation is required because he tapped into his existing mechanisms of human behavior. These are the things that have been built into his DNA from birth as a survival mechanism to keep him alive.

So when we go back to the analogy, what if you are standing 10 feet inside the entrance of the tunnel knowing that you have one action in front of you that you need to move past in order to move forward? For most people, the thought of this action is filled with the perception of discomfort and pain. You see someone you're attracted to and you're scared of rejection. You have to make that sales call with the nervousness of not knowing what to say. The pain of looking like a fool and failure. People are going to judge you if you don't get it right. If you're not perfect the first time around, your reputation could be ruined forever. Or God forbid, you have to run a mile or two on the treadmill at the gym. The pain is just so darn intense! So what is it going to take for you to do it?

Light the Fire Behind You

There's an old parable about conquistadors who set sail from Europe to conquer the Americas. Shortly after arriving in Central America, one of the leaders of the army ordered all of his soldiers off of the boats onto the land in front of them, with minimal supplies and weapons in hand. Once they were all safe ashore, he then ordered each ship's captain to burn the boats in the harbor behind them. Now, with no possible method of retreat, the soldiers had the fire lit within them where the only option was to move forward on their goals and succeed. If they didn't move forward towards their goals, with the lack of supplies and resources, they would die where they were. The fire has been lit and their emotions kicked into full-gear.

In 2012, I was down to the last $250 to my name and not making progress on my financial goals. I didn't build the internet business I wanted and I also wasn't motivated enough to even apply for jobs. I created my own version of Burning the Boats when I packed everything in my car and drove 2,000 miles across the country to Arizona. Now, when I was there, I needed to find a way to make it work because I didn't have the option to retreat. Not even enough money to afford gas to get home. And I did. I made it work. I wound up getting a customer service job that I hated, but it was a new life that was an upgrade from the unemployment years I had.

But after going to Arizona, a problem came. I still wanted to build my internet business but I was struggling to be motivated to take action. I followed all the advice I told you in this book so far. I set my destination and I chunked down everything to the one single step I needed to take in order to move forward on my goals. I needed to design the cover of my first magazine in Photoshop. I knew what I needed to do, I had no clue if it would work, but I knew that if I wanted any chance of building this business; it was one thing I needed to do. The problem: I still wasn't doing it.

What I want you to do now is create a numerical

comparison of two things. On one hand, is the thing you need to do. On the other hand, are the distractions that take you away from your goals. Rate each one in intensity and see which one is higher on the pain scale. Zero being no pain and ten being the most intense pain.

- **Doing the Magazine Cover -** On a scale of 1-10 - the intensity of pain associated with that action was a 7/10.
  - o The positive emotion factor was a 0/10. I feared wasting my time on something that would never pay off.
- **Procrastinating -** On the flip side, watching travel videos on YouTube had a pain factor of 0/10.
  - o The positive emotions I got from this were an 8/10.

So that was the one obstacle in the tunnel in front of me. In my perception, if I moved forward to do it, the pain would be a 7/10. I retreated out of the tunnel into the comfort of the light every single time.

But then I got a multi-millionaire mentor. A man who built multiple companies worth of $10 million each. He sold one of them for close to $60 million and was currently earning $75,000 per day with his new business. He gave me a piece of advice. The metaphorical equivalent of stepping into the tunnel and lighting a blazing fire behind me with the pain scale being a 10/10 if I didn't run forward FAST. Can you see how that with the pain behind me being a 10/10, this overpowered the 7/10 pain I felt from the magazine cover design, and I RAN FAST. In practical terms, we always move forward on the path of least resistance. In 2008-2009, I was a firefighter and one time I found myself on the second story of a building with the flames engulfed around me in the hallway and coming into the room I was in. Normal people don't jump out of windows, but when I had to retreat, I had to do what I had to do in order to avoid the more painful thing that was coming to get me.

The practical solution he gave me was to write a $100 check and hand it to my roommate. If I finished the magazine cover by midnight that same night, I would get the check handed back to me. If I didn't finish the magazine cover by the end of the night, my roommate would immediately cash the check and I would lose $100. All of a sudden, the act of procrastinating was a 10/10 in intensity and I moved forward on doing the 7/10 things from there. With my roommate holding the check, I had no option except to move forward because he would cash it if I gave up. Now, can you see how we setup this Burn the Boats forced accountability that lit the fire behind us to take action? Within the first few months of living together, my roommate built an internet business that was earning $45,000 per month. Another roommate of ours got $20,000 worth of sales within the first week of launching his product into the market. Eight months later, my internet business was making $10,000 per month with the 20 digital magazines I built using this forced accountability method. Before these destinations were reached, we saw many months of failure and no external results to motivate us along the way. It was this constant forced accountability that was needed in order to get us going.

I forgot if I mentioned that point to you before, but when someone goes to the gym, they won't see any external results for months. When building a business, it will be the same. Months or years go by where you put in the work that will pay off later. A delayed result. During this time of no external results, people often give up when they don't know they are on the right track. This is expected and those who keep going through it are the ones who reach the promised land.

So whatever it is. Going to the gym. Building a business. Writing a book. Or whatever your Now Step is, you can use this simple technique to all of a sudden make the idea of not taking action be more immediately painful than the action you need to take. The comfort of procrastination is no longer there. And when you hand it outside of your control, there's no backing out of it. This is the single most important thing I can't recommend enough if you've been struggling to take action. It's not the long-term effortless self-motivation I achieved by the end of this book, but it's enough to get you in motion.

Power-Ups Along the Pathway

On the flip side of that, let's now talk about the immediate desire for reward. In the Dopamine Traps chapter of this book, I talk about how app game developers create a system where it's a constant drip of rewards throughout the game. This is a way to stimulate the dopamine receptors in the brain to keep people addicted. When you do this correctly, it builds habits that stick. You play the game, you get rewarded. You stop playing the game and the reward goes away so you are immediately drawn back to what feels good now. The games don't always reward you for every action you take. The small losses you face when you fall down a pit or fail at a level trigger a desire for the reward to come back when you don't have it. But the game makes sure to give you enough easy rewards so you don't associate pain with playing the game (which would lead you to give up due to the bad feelings). There's also the unpredictability factor of the rewards so you don't grow accustomed to it in a pattern. If it happens predictably all the time, it'll get boring and the dopamine rush will go away. Casino slot machines are the same way. The same type of principles can apply to your motivation. Bells, whistles, flashing lights, and other noises are purposely built as triggers to cue you to take action.

The important thing, once again, is that it all has to deal with the emotions in the present moment. Not the desire for the goals in the future but the here and now. So how do we do this with relation to your habits and goals? Imagine the game super Mario Bros. Throughout the level, there are coins and power-up mushrooms that are sprinkled along the pathway to the end of the tunnel. For many people who

want
emot
place
leads
And
moti
into

N
go t
hous
part
It w
weig
rent
this
kno
they
exit

the form of positive rewards in
take the action and you get
people, the relief of the $10
them is enough, but wit
some other type of re

A Magnetic Force Pr
The next step of th
back to your Why fr
myself through a
of North Caro
police traini
the state
when
to

Monday, I would put in the work and be immediately rewarded after-the-fact with the 3-4 slices of pizza I grabbed on my way out. Outside of these Mondays, I went to the gym maybe once or twice a week. But every Monday, week after week, I made it to the gym at that exact time. Because my body was craving the immediate positive reward. While this may not be the best choice to eat 4 slices of pizza after the gym for weight loss goals, I did notice my muscle mass increased that summer. I found a way to make it to the gym regularly and I achieved my goals as my strength was improved. How can you apply this type of setup to your Now Steps? Sprinkle positive rewards that you crave immediately on the other side of the actions you take.

So, let's look at the tunnel for a moment again.

- **Immediate Pain -** You have the fire behind you. You chunk down to your Now Step, you light the fire with the $100 check method, and you're forced to move away from the pain and run forward.

- **Immediate Pleasure -** You have the power-ups in

front of you. You

rewarded. For many

0 check handed back to

the pizza from the gym -

ward can be powerful too.

ling You from the Future

e motivational driver process goes

m Chapter 2. In the fall of 2010, I put

elf-sponsored police academy. In the state

na, all police officers go through a 16-week

g program before applying for jobs throughout

Many years' prior, a man broke into my house

my sister and I were home alone at night, threatening

kill us. We called 911 and sometime later, a swarm of

police officers came rushing into the house, guns pointed, arrested the man, and saved our lives. From that moment forward, I knew that I wanted to be that type of person someday. To be able to come to people's aid when they are desperately in need. To help people through something that I struggled with in the past. So all throughout high school, I knew that my goal after graduation was to be a police officer. I didn't study as much as I should have during college because I knew that the degree I was getting wasn't required for this type of job. I often procrastinated on tasks and had more fun in college than study time.

But when I got accepted into one of the top police academies of the state, years later; I saw all of my career goals and dreams at the end of the long dark tunnel in front of me. I knew for a fact that going through this program was needed in order to achieve my goals. But it wasn't going to be an easy road in front of me. That tunnel was full of pain, struggle, and was comparable to marching through hell. I would have to wake up at 4:30 in the morning, drive an hour to the training center, with 2 hours of hard physical exercise in the morning, non-stop training, classes, and hands-on skills exercises throughout the day, with another hour of pushups on the burning hot parking lot ground during lunch, and then 2 more hours of physical exercise after classes ended at night. An hour drive home. Studying for the next day and making a perfectly clean and ironed uniform for the next day. If even so much as one thread was out of place, we would get punished and it would add more pain and struggle to our daily routine. All the while, I had no time for a part time job while in this program, and it provided no income for us at the time.

The intensity of this program was so difficult that 33% of the class dropped out within the first three days. Half of the class dropped out within the first week. But when we go back to the analogy of the tunnel, imagine as if the rewards of the pizza directly on the other side of the gym pulled me forward. It was a reward in the present moment that pulled me to the other side of the action I needed to take. The craving the food magnetically pulled me to the gym. While the natural programming of moving away from pain is a survival mechanism to keep us alive (built into our DNA), the food I crave is another one of the survival mechanisms built into our DNA. When we set up the right structure around these natural drivers, this is when motivation becomes a breeze. Imagine, like the pizza, that this magnetically pulled me forward through the action into the reward. The intensity of the desire on the other side could be a 9/10 and the pain of the action could be an 8/10. Because of the higher level of intensity for the reward, think of it as an emotional magnet that pulls you through the pain.

I mentioned earlier that our body only reacts to the emotions in the present moment. If the goal is too far away in the future, you most likely won't feel the pull that actually drives you forward through whatever it takes to get there. **Unless** that goal is powerful and emotionally charged enough to reach you in this present moment and pull you forward through the difficult tasks. For me, becoming a police officer was my biggest life goal at the time. No matter how much pain and struggle I faced in the tunnel, I felt the magnetism from the other side because it was a million-out-of-ten intensity which overpowered anything I would face to get there. This desire has to overpower the pain and fear you face. Through long hard days and even a trip to the emergency room for an injury I faced during the academy, I still pushed forward and never gave up, despite all the drivers of behavior in my body telling me to stop. It all boils down to the intensity of the emotions you feel. Is your Why powerful enough with a level of intensity where it makes all the pain and setbacks you face along the way irrelevant? If something is important enough to you and you feel the pull so strong coming through the tunnel - you'll do it. Even if you go through hell and back to get there.

Ultimately, there are a number of these natural drivers of behavior built into our DNA as survival mechanisms to keep us alive. Pain is a signal the body is destructing, so it pushes us to move away. Magnetism. The reward of food is the fuel that keeps us alive, so we move towards it. Another form of effortless magnetism. A mother would go through hell and back to save the life of her baby because there is another form of programming in our DNA to keep the human species alive. This is a type of programming that is more powerful than her self-preservation. In caveman tribes 10,000 years ago – if we didn't fit into the tribes we were in, we would be banished to the wilderness and die due to the lack of resources. This is why peer pressure is so effective and people assimilate to the people they spend the most amount of time with. Are you surrounding yourself with the right influences? Many people need the certainty that their energy is going into something that will pay off. In the days of food scarcity in the caveman wilderness, energy has to be preserved or your body will die when you don't get a meal during the famine. So when you doubt that you can achieve your goals, you'll naturally be pushed away and not even try. It is seen as wasted energy. You can work through this by reading inspirational success stories of people who achieved things from the ground up. Or you can flip the script and be certain that you'll be stuck in financial scarcity, loneliness, poor health, or in a place you don't want to be if you don't move forward. We also need excitement and variety. Similar to the uncertainty of the slot machine at the casino, if things get repetitive and predictable, we grow complacent – so it's important to switch up the routine from time to time.

Now, pay attention to these natural drivers of behavior. I listed some, but look at your real life experience. Do an online search for Maslow's Hierarchy of Needs for a complete list of them. What is needed to stay alive? How can you apply this to your motivational journey and what you need to do? Maybe surround yourself with people who already achieved your goals so you feel that need to be included in the tribe. Most of our programming has been built up for millions of years so it's better to make comparisons to the tribal days to see things from a new perspective. Your behavior will change naturally when you surround yourself with the right people like what happened to me when I took on that multi-millionaire mentor. But out of all these, there are the three that did it to me the most…

As you stand in the tunnel, there is your Now Step:

The Immediate Fire Behind You - The $100 Check Method is designed to work with your natural drivers of human behavior that keep you alive, like pulling your hand out of a fire, instinctually. And you can control this.

The Immediate Rewards in Front of You - The Pizza at the Gym (I'm Vegan Now :) - Just like an apple on a tree, all humans are pre-programmed to go towards immediate pleasure. When your tunnel is lined with coins, magic mushrooms, and power-ups, this creates the positive dopamine rush that keep you motivated with small wins along the way.

The Magnetism at the End of the Tunnel - Just like the police academy graduation, I finished #1 in my class because the thing at the end of the tunnel was so important to me - all the pain I faced along the way didn't matter anymore.

So, in summary, imagine seeing you standing at the

entrance of the tunnel. There is a bright light shining through from the other side which represents the intense emotional desires that magnetically pull you through even the hardest of times. When the goal is important enough to you, you will go through anything in order to get there. Ramp up the intensity of your desire. At the same time, fill the tunnel with coins and power-ups similar to a Super Mario Bros. game. And then light the fire behind you so you can Burn the Boats with the immediate pain of not taking action. When all of this is in place, you'll have everything you need in order to motivate yourself and succeed. So my suggestion for you is to choose one thing you know you need to do. And then hand $100 to a trusted friend and tell them you have to finish that task today, or else they keep it. When you finish it, have them hand it back to you. You feel the relief and reward for taking action. This is an important step to start building out a positive habit loop. When you reward yourself enough after a specific action, your brain begins to release the dopamine even if you don't get the positive reward. Thus, a habit is formed. Once you're done taking this step, chunk up, chunk down and repeat the process again with your new Now Step. Gym buddies are great for keeping you accountable. Mastermind groups are great for this in business. In future chapters of this book, I'll teach you more about building positive habits, as well as overcoming your fears of failure, rejection, doubt, and other blockages that prevent you from moving forward into the light.

Chapter 7

Overcome Your Fears

FAILURE, REJECTION, AND SUCCESS

Do you ever hesitate to take action because of a fear? It's like you're standing in a tunnel looking at your goals waiting for you on the other side. You see all the steps you need to take in front of you in order to get there. But there is an energetic force field that you have to walk through in order to take that next step. No matter how much you want to try, something is preventing you from moving forward and your fears keep holding you back.

- The fear of embarrassment
- The fear of rejection
- The fear of failure,
- The fear of ridicule, and
- Even the fear of success.

But contrary to what most people believe, it's not the thing that happens to you that you fear. Instead, it's the self-judgement you have for yourself if this fear unfolds. For example, two people could be laughed at and hung up on during a sales call. One of them beats himself up about it because he thinks he is a failure. Another person, given the exact same circumstances can brush it off and realize it's just a normal part of the process. Maybe the other person had a bad day? It has nothing to do with him. No big deal. Which one of those two people are more likely to move forward with their goals? The one without the self-judgement, of course.

Remember this one thing: It all boils down to self-judgement about who you are if this fear unfolds. "If I move forward and try this, and (this fear unfolds), it means I am (not good enough/a loser/a reject/etc.)". Regardless of whatever type of external judgement you might face from others, it's time to focus inward. When you learn how to remove this self-judgement and don't take things personally, then you release the deepest part of the emotional blockage. The force field is open and ready for you to step forward.

The Fear of Success

I'll start off by demonstrating the fear of success. Many years ago, I worked with a client who wanted to start a website design business. Something inside was holding him back from cold calling local businesses and offering his services to them. It was like he was standing in a tunnel with an invisible force field in front of him, not letting him move forward with his goals. He described an emotion in his stomach that was like an energetic chord, holding him back. No matter how much he logically tried to overcome his fears, he still wouldn't make those calls.

The way the process works: Looking forward into the future, he unconsciously sees two potential pathways if he takes action on this task.

1. **Path 1 –** He gets rejected on the sales call and the worst-case scenario happens.
2. **Path 2 –** He has success and closes the sale for $5,000

Was it the fear of failure? No, not in this case. He came from a background where he faced many failures in other areas of his life and it wasn't so much that. But what he was facing instead was a fear of success. The very first step of the process is to bring up a clear picture of what that fear would look like as if it already unfolded. So I had him bring up a picture in his mind, envisioning that he already made those cold calls, he already sold $5,000 websites to local businesses, and he already achieved his financial success. When I asked him to describe that visual representation to me, he told me that he was standing in his parents' house, surrounded by his family. Somehow, in that picture, they all were judging him because they saw him as a greedy person. As myself, and many other entrepreneurs know - a website redesign by somebody who knows what they are doing could only take a couple of days to complete. When he wanted to place the $5,000 price tag on it, he had the internal guilt that he was ripping people off because he equated the value he delivered with the amount of time it would take him. Not with the end benefits to the client. So, in his mind, can you see the clear self-judgement he would face if he achieved his goal. Regardless of how his family reacted in his mind, it goes back to the self-judgement. "If I move forward and (sell this website design package), and (this business owner pays me $5,000), it means I am a (greedy person)". What many people don't know is that visual I had him bring up in his mind is his self-image from the part of the brain directly responsible for his behavior. That visual image of who he is was filled with emotions. And that right there is the root of the emotional force field that I was talking about. Behind the scenes of his conscious awareness, all of this information was being computed automatically. Simply the act of making the phone call would result in a chain of events that led to that self-judgement. So the force field was created.

Just like a lot of things in Deconstructing Motivation, can you see how the structure of this process is the same, regardless of the content. He brings up a visual in his mind, seeing himself in the picture as if that fear unfolded. You find out what the self-judgement is and then you use a rapid emotional release technique to get rid of the emotional blockage that holds many people back.

During our session, we went through a technique to release the buildup of emotions and we also redefined the picture in his mind to release the self-judgement. Yes, for somebody who knows how to design websites like him, it is a quick job. But the average customer value of the business he was selling to is $2,000. So if that website he made creates even three more sales over the next year for the business owner he works with - that is a profitable investment. The business owner (who is a blue collar worker by trade - and has no online knowledge), is not paying for his time, he is paying for his years of expertise learning how to code websites. He is paying for more sales and the results he gets. If this website brings in 2 more sales per month - than that is $4,000 more income per month for a man who is currently losing out on a lot of potential customers with an under-performing website. In fact, if my client went in and achieved those results for the man, he would be happy and would be glad to recommend his friends to this client of mine as well.

Now, after re-defining this picture in his mind, the self-judgement of being a greedy person was gone. He shifted the image to a picture of him stepping into his potential of helping improve local businesses in his community. He could offer a money-back guarantee, meet people in person to build up more trust, and be an honest person by holding to his word. He now sees himself as a respected member of the community.

It all revolves around the picture he has in his mind.

All of a sudden, by looking at the same outcome in a different perspective, it releases that emotional blockage that prevented him from moving forward. After our session, he made his first three cold calls by the end of the day. Did he go on and close the sale for that business? I don't know, because learning sales is a journey in itself, but at least he overcame his fear of success and started making the cold calls.

While many people go out there and preach people to push through their fears, I spent years working with aspiring entrepreneurs and salespeople to go through this process to remove the things that many people feel hold them back: Nothing more but thoughts (pictures in their mind) and (emotions) attached to this. This part of the mind does not respond to logic, but it responds to pictures and emotions.

Look at it this way...

Pushing through your fears is like somebody telling you to go climb over an electric fence that will most likely electrocute you. This is the process of turning off the electricity that charges the fence so you can hop over it with ease.

The Behavior-Generating Part of the Human Mind

There are three parts of the human mind. The conscious mind, the unconscious mind, and the higher self. The unconscious mind is "The Other 90%" of the brain that traditional thinking says we don't have access to. It is the part of our brain where habits are stored and is directly responsible for human behavior. The unconscious mind also thinks in pictures and symbols. So while he couldn't pinpoint the exact fear of what was holding him back, I told him to bring up a picture in his mind of the fear, allow what picture comes to him, and then see himself in the picture. When we make a change in this part of the mind, it creates an instant change in our behavior. Both with our mental perception (seeing himself as a greedy person) and the emotions tied to it (feeling that blockage 8/10 intensity in the pit of his stomach). This same process of overcoming your fear of success also helps overcome your fear of failure, embarrassment, and ridicule.

A warning of safety: Please note that this process should be done with a trained professional because there are some fears that are there for a reason and serve to protect us. Nobody wants to overcome a fear of jumping out of an airplane without a parachute and many of our behaviors are held in place as protective mechanisms. I simply share these stories to show you that there is an easier way out there to move through things that hold many people back forever. For fears that don't have an impact on your safety, it's a good first step to just re-frame that picture in your mind.

The Fear of Failure/Rejection/Ridicule

Many years ago as a young man, I used to have a lot of nervousness and anxiety around women that I found attractive. I would see someone I was attracted to, immediately place her out of my league, and the fear built up to the point where it paralyzed me and I couldn't even talk to her. The process that I used to overcome this fear is the same as the fear of success. I would think of the thing I was avoiding doing (talking to the woman I found attractive) and then bring up a picture in my mind of the worst-case scenario if I go talk to her. Seeing myself from the third person perspective, I would see her blowing me off, people all around would be pointing and laughing at me, and I would see myself as a loser. No matter how much logical thinking and advice that came my way saying this wouldn't happen, it was this image in my mind that prevented me from doing it - because of the self-judgement of who I was in the picture. I saw myself as being a loser. The emotions I felt connected to this were a 10/10. So in the same way my client worked through the fear of success by redefining the picture in his mind, I have grown more over the years to permanently redefine these pictures in my mind for most things I do.

When Circumstances Shift Your Perception

In the fall of 2016, I spent three months traveling through Europe and one day found myself at a Moroccan Tea Shop on the southern coast of Spain. With the place almost full during lunch hour, there was one table left next to this very attractive woman. My social anxiety kicked in and I almost didn't go there because of the nervousness to sit next to her. I eventually sit down and order my tea. As I overhear her talking on the phone in English (not so common in Spain) about business (an interest of mine); she eventually hung up the phone and I asked her if she is from the United States. She responded "No" in an Eastern European accent, acting closed off, and I felt as if she was judging me for event talking to her. I apologized and just made a comment that I'm a business owner and I'm traveling so I found what she was talking about interesting. All of a sudden, she opened up and we had a great conversation. Later on, I found out that she is an international model that has a large following of men online. She constantly finds herself being harassed by sleazy men and has grown so annoyed with this. She even had to change her name online to protect her identity. The moral of the story? When she first gave me the cold shoulder, I took it personally. My thoughts of being a loser, unconfident, and judged were the root of the whole problem with myself-confidence. Remember what I said before? It all comes down to self-judgement. I could go up to her to say hi, be rejected, and view it as something personal about me, which would lead to the negative emotions paralyzing me by fear. Or, I could remember the lesson from this experience and see that it means nothing personal about me and see that her, and countless of other women like her, have to deal with so many guys that harass them. As a result, they have a natural, automatic defense mechanism to protect their time, energy, and safety. When a normal person like me comes up - it's just her natural defense mechanisms kicking in. When you don't take rejection personally - the fear is no longer holding you back.

Ever since this instance going forward, I've been rejected by people many times. But when I remind myself that it doesn't mean anything bad about me, this provides me the emotional balance to no longer block myself from even trying.

While the example I used was with my dating life from years ago, I also noticed that this process made a significant improvement on my ability to handle rejection and failure in business and other areas of my life as well. Do you fear being judged by going to the gym for the first time when you are fat? Or running slow on a track when so many people around you are already in shape? Do you fear failing on an essay for school because it's not perfect? You know, the people who do the most judging are the ones who are so down with their own lives, they have nothing better to do than to pull other people down like crabs in a bucket who are trying to rise up and do great things. All of the people who I go to the gym with have respect for people who are out of shape and have the motivation to start exercising. Or if you cold call 10 potential clients for selling your services. They scream at you, they curse at you, they say you are spamming them. With the understanding that they are just not the right fits and if you truly believe in what you're selling - there are many people out there who are waiting for someone like you to come into their lives and give them a solution to their problems.

With the self-judgement and taking it personally - the fear is there holding you back from even trying it again. I'm sure you can count at least a hundred experiences like this from your entire life. These significant emotional events from the past build up and cause even further blockages to form around the seed that has been planted. But when you take the lessons learned from this chapter, it helps reduce the force field so those blockages are gone.

So, in most instances, it's a mental game tied to pictures and emotions that are like an invisible force field holding you back due to your fears. When it's an irrational fear - simply ask yourself what is the worst case scenario if you fail and/or succeed. Allow a picture to come up in your awareness. See yourself in the picture. Re-define the picture to not take things personally and release the self-judgement. See yourself in a different light. This is the process I followed with hundreds of clients and using the tools and techniques I learned over the years - overcoming fears usually takes about 20-30 minutes. Sometimes they come back for a bit, and other times they are gone forever.

Those are irrational fears. Fears that don't have a direct impact on your safety. Being face-to-face with a mother moose protecting her child is a real fear that should be avoided. Going through dangerous parts of other countries late at night are generally rational fears that should be avoided. Jumping out of an airplane without a parachute is a rational fear that should be avoided. So if the worst-case-scenario is one that could put your physical safety and/or well-being at risk, don't mess with the part of you that is being protected. Also, if you face any internal resistance of working through a fear (a gut feeling that you shouldn't change something, etc.), don't do it because there are more complexities at work here.

But if it means picking up a phone, asking someone out, or taking a leap to a new job; the process I outlined for you can help. It releases the force field that often is tied up in your stomach, holding you back from moving forward. Fear of failure. Fear of rejection. Fear of success. Re-define who you are in the picture mentally, and don't take it personally.

Fear of Staying the Same

I mention in most of my books that the best part of my life began when I was down to the last $250 to my name, I just spent the past two years unemployed and broke living on the East Coast, and drove 2,000 miles across the country to have lunch with a millionaire I met on the internet. For most people, taking such a leap into the darkness would be a risk. But I wasn't moving forward with the dreams I committed to with being an internet entrepreneur. Life was getting worse for me by the day. I soon learned that the biggest fear many of us should have is what happens if we don't step forward, take this leap; and our life forever remains the same. Many people are not happy where they are but have no clue how amazing life can be when they see nothing but a positive vision on the other side.

Ask yourself this question: When you do that thing you fear, what picture or movie plays through your mind? Do you see it leading only to failure? Or can you bring up a bright, crystal-clear vision of the best-case possible outcome?

Looking at the Bright Side

When I took that leap of faith, I maxed out my $500 limit credit card with gas and hotels on my way there and gambled my last $250 in a game of poker. I won $2,000 during that game, got a low-wage customer service job, and secured housing within the first month. Things worked out and I spent the next few years of my life feeling like I was living in a dream vacation in Scottsdale, Arizona. Palm trees, sunshine, so many great people, and awesome things every day. This was compared to the lack of all social life in the small farm town of less than 1,000 people I moved from. I was scared to leave. Often times, like when I was scared to talk to women I found attractive, or I was scared to make phone calls to sell my services for my business; we only look at the worst-case scenario and we can't envision the successful outcome as even an option. So many self-development coaches (including myself) guide clients through detailed visualization processes that allow them to reframe their negative mindset into a positive one so they can see the good things that come on the other side. So what if instead of focusing on all the bad things that could happen and the "What if...'s" that my parents lectured me about before I drove across the country, we focus on the positive? I went from risk-adverse, to risk-taker.

Getting a Little Too Reckless

For many years, I was living in that fear-free mindset. After building my first internet business, I was still scared to quit the safety and security of my corporate job and travel like I wanted to. So I did some work to get through this fear, I was Standing on the Edge of Darkness and I jumped. I quit my job, packed my car in Scottsdale, and then spent the next few years traveling the United States, living in many different cities. Then, years later, I took that leap again and packed everything I could in a travel backpack and decided to travel through Europe for three months straight. I took risks when I shouldn't. I spent the last of the money I had in my bank account on one cold dark rainy night in the middle of Manchester United Kingdom. Coincidentally, that same moment the ATM declined my card, my cell phone service cut off, the man I was staying with got in a drunk angry rage after a bad day at work, and threw everything I owned on the street while I was out on a date. No money. No cell phone. 10:30 at night. Dark foreign country. I spent the next week living with my date eating ramen noodles and cheap wine. After that, I spent three weeks couch surfing with an Eastern European Dominatrix in the middle of Amsterdam's Red Light District while I got myself back on track. It was a one hell of an experience that makes a great story for another book, but it really put me in a bad position when my fears actually came true.

- On one hand, I used to be filled with fear and stayed in my comfort zone. I didn't enjoy my experiences and I held myself back from going after my dreams.
- On the other hand, I removed all of my fears, lived some really amazing experiences in this life, and was left in a bad position when my fears came true.

So instead of being all the way to the left on the scale or all the way right, there is a way to find the right balance of both.

Creating a Stop-Loss and a Balance

In those instances, I learned there needs to be a perfect balance between overcoming your fears altogether, risk-avoidance, and taking more calculated risks. Many people who are not motivated are reading this now and lean more on the safe side. That is why I started off the chapter with the method for taking a clear look at the worst-case scenario. If it's a rational fear that could lead to danger, don't mess with it. If it's an irrational fear, release the self-judgement about who you are if that unfolds (don't take it personally), re-define the picture in your mind, release the emotions; and then this opens up the portal so you can step through that gateway of the invisible force field and move forward down that tunnel towards your goals. Fear of failure and fear of success alike. I spent many months working through a lot of my fears that have been building up within me my entire life and made myself 100% completely (emotionally) ok if the worst case scenario unfolded. By doing that, I placed myself in very bad situations, such as running out of money in a foreign country, facing ridicule by others, and many of those fears actually did come true in my life.

But when they did, I was left in a place of peace.

It's almost as if I let out a big sigh of relief that the fear unfolded and it actually wasn't as bad as I thought. As a young healthy man who allowed this to happen to him in his late 20's with no mortgage, family to take care of, and as a personal development coach who can handle the adversity - I made it through to the other side stronger than I ever was before. I wouldn't trade these experiences for anything.

But for many people reading this, some fears if they unfold - you can be in a good emotional position if you face them (nothing holding you back from taking action), and if you get a little too reckless - it can have a very negative impact on your life.

So I view things like this: At the bottom of the skyscraper is the worst-case scenario. What is the worst possible thing that could happen if you try this and fail? See that for what it is and don't suppress it. On the top of the skyscraper is the best-case scenario if you move forward and you succeed. When you build the confidence in yourself that you can achieve the greatest success and you remove your fears, you are emotionally equipped to walk up all the flights of stairs to reach the top, and you'll be emotionally ok if you don't.

But in the middle, it's important to put a stop-loss. A stop loss is an industry term for people who trade stocks. I'm not a stock trader myself, but from my understanding of it; you can buy a stock at $40 per share. Let's say you buy 1,000 shares for a total investment of $40,000. You're optimistic the company you invested in will succeed and the price could go up to $50 per share (a $10,000 profit for you at $50,000). If you put your life savings in the stock, and you're motivated to move forward on this - three things could happen.

1. **The stock stays the same.** You neither make money nor lose money.
2. **The stock goes up.** You make the money and you achieve your goal.
3. **The stock begins to crash** suddenly before you are even alerted at this. Perhaps a news article comes out that the CEO of the company was indicted on fraud charges and the company is on the brink of collapse.

Without a stop-loss, your life savings of $40,000 could go down to $0 really quickly and you'd hit rock bottom. You are fearless so your reckless actions led you to this. But with a stop-loss, you can have the computer automatically pull your money out if the stock price hits $35 per share. You took a loss of $5,000, but it's not the end of the world. You have time to go back and recalibrate to try again. A stop-loss is an objective milestone that alerts you that it's time to move back.

So the same holds true with what you're working on. You set a positive vision you move towards, you align yourself internally with optimism, you overcome your fears of failure/success, and then you have a stop-loss in place that is not emotion-based, but objective, so you can withdraw before things start spiraling out of control.

I've had a lot of experiences of failures and successes in my life and this formula has been the most effective for me so far. I started on one side of the spectrum (super risk-adverse), then I went to fearless (reckless), and then balanced out in the middle.

Stepping into Your Fears

On a final note, what if you don't have to overcome your fears in order to move forward towards your goals? Instead, what if you train yourself to no longer allow these emotions you feel to hold you back, but instead you harness the power of them and allow this energy to be a force that propels you forward. After all, the motivation you use in this world is harnessing the emotions you feel within your body. And this energy of fear is a very powerful one. When you learn how to channel it correctly, it can turn that force field in front of you into an energetic booster that instantly propels you to the next level. What happens if, when you step through it, you'll be blown away by what amazing things are waiting just out of sight on the other side? Many people don't see the success that is waiting for them just out of sight.

Change the pictures in your mind.

But my biggest fear always remains the same.

What if you never even try to work towards your goals and your life continues to remain the same? What if you spend your whole life struggling financially because you don't go after that promotion or build that business? What if you continue to eat unhealthy and you die early of a disease? That's the bigger risk. If you don't even try to move forward because of your fears. Much scarier than the short-term failures you may face along the way. In perspective, those aren't even failures to begin with. It's just a natural learning curve everybody goes through to learn and grow from; to make you better. Comfort keeps you alive. Stepping into the darkness and getting your emotions going is often times what it takes in order to thrive.

But, even with your fears gone, what happens when you actually do face these failures, obstacles, and setbacks along the way?

Chapter 8

Obstacles & Setbacks

THE JOURNEY TO SUCCESS IS LINED WITH A THOUSAND FAILURES ALONG THE WAY

Often times we feel like we're not headed in the right direction and things aren't going according to plan. We have this picture in our mind of the exact path we created to reach our goals. We have expectations that everything will always go right. But then reality hits us in the face and we are confronted with obstacles, failures, and setbacks along the way. This causes a lot of people to feel discouraged and give up. Do you know that old saying, "It simply wasn't meant to be"? Too many people live by this phrase as absolute truth and it causes them to turn around and try something else. But what if they simply didn't try hard enough and gave up too soon? Imagine for a moment that you're standing on a trail and you have to move forward in order to reach the top of the mountain. A large boulder is right in front of you and it's blocking your path. In this moment, you have three options:

1. Push through it with force,
2. Take another path, or
3. Give up and walk away.

Which one of those options will get you to the top of

the mountain the quickest? I'm a big fan of getting to the root cause of problems that hold us back from achieving our goals. If you give up and walk back to the bottom of the mountain, you're simply not doing what it takes to be successful. You avoided the temporary problem, but you didn't master the lesson and the skill of moving past obstacles so you can actually move forward on your path. What happens when you face another obstacle with something else in the future? Do you give up again? No matter what you do in life, there will always be obstacles you have to overcome. Instead, what if you mastered the ability to remove these obstacles and choose the best course of action so future problems are nothing more than a breeze to move past? Can you see the difference between getting to the root cause of problems (mastering the skill) vs. simply moving away from the surface-level problem (this one obstacle)?

The first step of the process is to get out of fairytale land and have the proper expectations of what your journey to success will actually look like.

Reasonable Expectations

What I learned from my journey towards achieving great things in my life is that every failure you face is a normal part of the process. Sometimes these obstacles we face are simply something we need to push through. A person doesn't meet their soulmate when asking only one person on a date. You have to go through a hundred first dates before you find the right one. When seeking investment money for a company we are in, one of my team members had to follow up with a potential investor 27 times (through non-returned phone calls, disappearances, etc.) before securing the funding we need from him. In those instances, it's a matter of pushing forward through the obstacle and getting to the other side. Persistence is the name of the game. If you can't push the boulder off of the trail, it might take another strategy to blow through it with a piece of dynamite. While the strategies and methods you use to get through this obstacle vary, these are all methods to push through it with brute force. Other times, a string of failures we face are a sign we should re-adjust the course and head in a new direction. The destination is the same, so you're not giving up. There might be a new trail that branches off from where you are as a detour to get there faster. Finally, after all resources are drained, it might actually be a sign to give up. I repeat, after all resources are drained. Not when you face some adversity here and there. That's an option always left best for last. Or never. But how do we know which one of those three options to choose from?

A Story of Taking a New Path to the Same Goal

In 2015, I set a goal to be published in a major industry magazine. Months later, I received an email from one of the editors of Inc. Magazine, one of the largest entrepreneur magazines out there, saying they wanted to do a feature on me. I replied to the editor, months went by, and I completely forgot about their promise to consider me for publication. During that same time, my app business took a toll for the worst. An algorithm updated and virtually all of my apps lost their first-position rankings. This caused sales to drop quickly. Facing such a tremendous loss and financial setback along the way, I began facing a serious buildup of anxiety and stress. Mixed with my lavish spending and maxing out my credit cards every month, the income that could pay for all of that was suddenly gone and I wasn't sure how I could even pay rent. At the time, I was renting out a place in a wooded area by the Puget Sound of Seattle, thousands of miles away from my friends and family members. I began experiencing heart palpitations, night sweats, and other surface-level symptoms as a result of an unsafe buildup of stress.

At the time, I was building up a new company that trains other entrepreneurs how to start and grow their businesses. I created training programs on everything from The Fundamentals of Entrepreneurship, Mindset, Motivation, Finding a Business Idea, Sales, and Marketing. At the same time, this magazine finally published the article about me. In the article, they talk about how I pay my freelance employees from the Philippines $4 per hour. This is double their traditional working wage for most people there, but people in the US don't see this and they saw me as a terrible person. Many pro-American, anti-globalism people flooded my inbox with hate mail, death threats, and calling me the worst human being on the face of the earth. When one person says something bad about you, it hurts. When a rumor gets spread about you in a circle of friends, at work, or at school; it hurts even more. But having hundreds of people hating your very existence, it became too much to handle. Mixed with the existing stress I had, I knew it was time for a change.

When Things Don't Go According to Plan

I found myself rushing to the emergency room on many occasions due to the medical problems from stress. I was in and out of doctors' offices all winter, thinking something was seriously wrong with me at the time. When searching on the internet, I found all sorts of different symptoms and diseases that I thought I had. Time and time again, it all boiled down to having too much stress.

People told me entrepreneurship was not an easy journey, but I had no clue what I was in store for. Before getting into this, I just used to see people on the internet have money flow effortlessly into their bank account when they put up a website. Nobody out there talked about the real struggles we as entrepreneurs face.

Just months prior, I was filming YouTube videos, traveling all across the country, promoting positivity and here I was – lying face down in my bed for months straight unable to escape from the emotional pain. I was not motivated myself, and in my mind, everything was going off course.

I had my path laid out ahead of me, I worked through my fears that prevented me from moving forward, and then after all that; I had all the confidence and motivation to move forward with my goals, but life handed me a dose of reality. At the time, I thought it took me off course. How does somebody who lays face down in his bed for three months straight lead a movement of people for motivation and emotional balance? I was too stressed to work on my business, I was too down on life to exercise, take care of my eating, or stay in shape. By the look of everything on the outside, I was falling completely off course.

I set the course out for myself and then an obstacle comes my way where nothing is going according to the plan. It is usually in this moment where people think that it wasn't meant to happen or it's time to give up. Other people hold onto their motivation, but they continue marching off in the wrong direction instead of the new path that they are supposed to be walking on. We can't control everything that happens to us along the way. What a great way to end 2015.

As January 2016 rolls around, I continue in this downward spiral eventually with a doctor handing me a bottle of anti-depressants to boost chemical levels in my brain and cover up the stress. I don't know how it works, but the side effects of this drug were worse than the symptoms I was facing. If I gave up on the drug too soon, one of the side effects could potentially lead to death. In that moment, I was faced with a decision. Should I continue forward with the spiral I was on? Or should I surrender to where life was pushing me and maintain my motivation to blindly move forward, with faith that I should really be stepping forward on a new path?

I threw the bottle of pills in the garbage, mustered up the motivation to do some graphic design services for money, and then searched for a natural solution. On my way back from Seattle to the East Coast, I drove through the city of Boulder, Colorado where I stayed with my friend Scott for a few days. We went hiking through the foothills of the Rocky Mountains and something about the atmosphere of the city was so relaxing. I just knew in my core, that I had to go back. So I packed up my car once again with a new journey, and a new mission in life to find a natural solution to balance my emotions and naturally handle the stress.

My journey led me to a man named Jim, a psychologist who ran a meetup group teaching techniques for natural solutions to stress. My golden ticket was here. For months on end, I studied under his mentorship and began to learn natural ways to deal with these hard and troubling obstacles we face in life. Most notably, he taught me a technique called EFT – The Emotional Freedom Technique, where you use your fingers to repeatedly tap on energetic pathways in your body while you focus on a specific negative emotion. The tapping disrupts the energy flow and releases it from your neurology. Like pouring out a cup of water, in the matter of 30 minutes, virtually all of my stress was gone. I continued my mentorship deeper with NLP and learned how to connect with the very core of our being. Not only to drain the plague of stressful emotions from our body, but to fill it with the flow of life so they don't come back.

A Lesson About "Negative" Emotions

While in Colorado, I found myself backpacking one summer afternoon through Rocky Mountain National Park. On that trail, myself and a friend of mine went face-to-face with an angry mother moose trying to protect her baby. My body filled with stress and anxiety. In that moment, there were no negative emotions, but simply emotional signals that are pushing us in a certain direction. The emotions that filled my body put me into fight or flight mode and caused me to do the things I needed to do in order to survive. Climbing 11,000 feat high above a glacier, I faced freezing cold, cramps, and dangerous predators when night began to fall as we were rushing to hike our way back to vehicle four miles out of the wilderness below. In that moment, I learned that many fears we have are rational, and it's best to not let our emotions build up, get out of control, but to utilize them as our greatest resource, and let things flow. In those instances, the stress led me to the safety of the car.

That story I shared is at the micro-level. But more often

in life, we build up with a subtler sense of stress and anxiety when we are not meant to be where we are. Perhaps the stress you feel is pointing you to do something new in your life? And to stop doing something else? Listen to your emotions, get to the root cause of things, see where they are pointing you, and the magical transformations happen from there.

During this "detour" on my pathway to the top, I also began learning so many things about becoming a psychic, manifesting with the Law of Attraction, out of body experiences, and everything to do with spirituality. In many spiritual teachings, they say there is a higher power that is guiding us through life. Your higher self, God, Allah, the universe, fate, karma, or whatever you call it – this is a part of you that sees the pathways that you should be walking on even when you don't. A part of yourself that hands you opportunities just out of sight when you need them the most, and always has your best intent and interest in mind. I've jumped face first into the unknown on many occasions. Each and every time when I reached my darkness hour, an opportunity is waiting just out of sight. Whether I was motivated to take it or not was a decision I could choose to make.

It's now years later, and I no longer get stressed out by the obstacles and struggles in life that used to plague me so much in the past. Things come up, but it was only through this experience I faced, after taking massive action, before I learned the real lessons on how to handle this myself. I am able to have the proper expectations that things don't go according to plan along the way. I have the sensory acuity to notice when I'm heading along the wrong track, I have the proper persistence to know when it's not a sign to give up, as well as the behavioral flexibility to find a new path and acquire the resources to shift gears and change when its' required. There's probably a formula for this somewhere, but I view this skillset more as an artistic dance, instead of scientific in form.

The end result is my ability to help other people navigate through virtually all of the struggles we face in the inner game of life. I published this experience into a book called The Journey for Lasting Happiness – Timeless Secrets to a Stress-Free Life. I've coached many people to help them pull out of stressful and difficult times, to help them enjoy their experiences the same. I also applied these lessons to better understand how our emotional state impacts motivational levels, and how to quickly pull out of dark stressful times. It was through these experiences, obstacles, setbacks, and massive failures that I faced where I developed the skills needed to be more effective at what I do. These are things you can't learn from reading a book alone.

Bad things happen in life, but the moral of this story is that many times we may expect to go down one path in life, thinking it's the only trail we have. Obstacles, setbacks, and roadblocks come up; which throw us off course and many people feel like giving up. If it wasn't for this new path, I wouldn't be in the much better position I am today. I never saw this at the beginning of the trail. Only in hindsight.

Maybe the same holds true for you?

The Reasonable Expectations You Should Face

Odds are that most of your setbacks, failures, and obstacles you face on your journey don't cause you to go on a crazy adventure spanning three continents, tens of thousands of miles, and eight different countries like mine did. Maybe you face larger failures and obstacles than me. Maybe they are different in nature, but similar in structure. The athlete training for years on end, only to suffer a broken bone and an injury as a setback that stops them in their tracks.

When I was building my first business, the magazine publishing company, I used to avoid failure every step of the way. When submitting my first magazine app to Apple, it was rejected 16 times straight. Each and every time, I wanted to jump ship and set a new course by doing something else, thinking that this wasn't part of the plan. As I mentioned earlier in this book, because I pushed through these obstacles, I eventually built that company up to 1.3 million readers years down the road. Can you see the importance of having one clear destination and a powerful Why that glues you on course through these failures?

While I was facing that problem, my roommate was having trouble finding a manufacturer to produce the products he was selling from home. Every night, orders would line up and he spent 8 hours fulfilling them. His time was drained making his products instead of growing his business through advertising. He procrastinated with finding a manufacturer for months on end until he made the decision to make 100 cold calls, expecting 100 people to say no. The only mission was to make the calls and get to the other side. Success/failure/rejection was no longer part of the expectation he had. It was simply to hit 100 cold calls. After 37 people said no, the 38th one finally said yes. Because he freed up his time to advertise more, his business grew from $12,000 to $45,000 per month within the next 20 days. Can you see how shifting his expectations shifted his behavior and ultimately led to his results?

Instead of thinking that the things you face are signs that you're on the wrong track, see if it's simply a rock in the middle of the river where you can shift gears a little bit and effortlessly flow around. Think of it as the stream of life. When my app was rejected because one line of code was bad, I made the adjustment, resubmitted, and it was rejected for another reason that was different this time. I adjusted, re-submitted, and another reason came up, which broke the first fix I made at the start. In NLP training, they say there is no failure, only feedback. I was reading an article this morning that quoted Jeff Bezos, the billionaire founder of Amazon who spoke on the topic:

"Take risk. You have to be willing to take risk. If you have a business idea with no risk, it's probably already being done," he said, according to an Amazon transcript. "You've got to have something that might not work. It will be, in many ways, an experiment." Many of those experiments will fail, but "big failures" are a necessary part of the journey toward success, he said. "We take risks all the time, we talk about failure," he said. "We need big failures in order to move the needle. If we don't, we're not swinging enough. You really should be swinging hard, and you will fail, but that's okay."

The journey to success is filled with a million obstacles. These are the types of results you see when you have the proper expectations about obstacles, setbacks, and roadblocks on your journey. Don't let it take away from your motivation, but simply embrace it as a sign that you're on the right path. Keep moving forward, because feedback (not failure) is the only sign you're moving.

Short Term Speed Bumps vs. Long Term Failure

I'd like to finish this chapter with a piece of advice. Many people don't understand the reasonable expectations it takes when you set out to motivate yourself to do larger things in life. They expect the trail to be full of rainbows and butterflies. But on the journey to success, it is riddled with short-term failures (speed bumps) along the way. You can make 100 cold calls for your business and 99 of them will say no, but that one that says yes is what you're going for. Even if 100 say no, you can build up your skills so you'll do better on the next hundred. I once spent six months coding a website that nobody signed up for. I can now code a website and sales page in the matter of hours when I start a new online business or want to promote a new book. When I built my iOS app publishing company, my apps were rejected 16 times before the first one was approved. I wanted to give up every single time. I faced a hundred different similar setbacks along the way. I went on 100 first dates before I met the love of my life. Embrace short-term failure because it's normal. Even if my business fails in the long term, it puts me in a much better position than if I didn't even move forward and do anything - because of all the experience I gained. Experience and skills that will last me a lifetime, so I do it better the next time around.

So I'd like to finish this chapter with a few pieces of parting advice. In summary, keep moving forward because the obstacles you face are normal. There is no failure, only feedback.

It is important to recognize the things you are doing wrong and to have the flexibility to adjust along the way. The same actions that worked in the past may not be the same things you do in the future. It's an art, not a science. Try new things and you'll get new results. What if you try to fail 100 times so one day you accidentally don't fail, and wind up succeeding? The only way you get this feedback is to move forward with a lot of actions quickly, instead of standing in place. You may struggle from short-term failures, but the biggest fear you should have is the long-term vision of never moving forward with your goals and life continuing to remain the same.

Now go out there, and get that feedback!

DECONSTRUCTING MOTIVATION

Chapter 9

The Habit Loop

BUILDING POSITIVE ACTIONS, HABITS, AND DAILY ROUTINES THAT STICK!

Up until this point of the book, you've been provided with everything you need in order to move forward and achieve your goals. You can set your destination, break it down into it's very specific action-steps, narrow your focus on one, and utilize your body's existing natural drivers of motivation so it becomes virtually effortless. This in itself is more than enough to start taking action. If you're reading this book for personal development, it's all you really need. But if you're reading this book for more academic knowledge, or peak performance strategies, it's time to go deeper into that. You also got introduced to some more advanced motivational psychology about re-defining the pictures in your mind as a way to help release the force field of fears that prevent you from stepping forward. In the upcoming chapters of the book, I'd really like to switch gears for a second. Before reading this book, you didn't know how to motivate yourself. Now you do. So the next stage of your journey, with the existing knowledge you have, it is time to take your motivation to the next level. These are some of the more advanced strategies I use to take motivated individuals and allow them to reach peak performance levels with optimal drive, focus, and energy. Just like Setting Your Destination where all arrows are pointing in one direction to the center of a target, everything in the upcoming chapters of this book should point towards one thing: The greatest amount of energy channeled into the actions you should be taking. And removing the blockages that limit it, distractions that deflect it off course, as well as other things that drain it away.

The first step is conscious awareness.

The Behavior Comparison Chart

When you started to find your path, you began making a checklist of all the actions you should start taking in order to lead you towards your goals. But on the flip side of that is also conscious awareness of the negative behaviors that take time and energy away from them. Perhaps you want to eat healthier but you find yourself always eating potato chips. You want to work on your business but you always find yourself browsing through social media. So the first thing you should do is start creating a list with two columns on a piece of paper. On the left are the actions you should be taking each day. On the right are the actions that are taking time and energy away from your goals. Call this one your exclusionary list. While I am a true believer of living a well-balanced life and not all of your energy should go into your primary goal all of the time; make a point to write down the list of things you normally do but want to stop completely. Also circle things you might not want to eliminate, but reduce the amount of time you put into them. Maybe you can be productive during the day and watch an hour or two of TV at night. Or if you really want to cut out television, make sure that stays on the exclusion list. With this list, you have a clear understanding of what you should and shouldn't be doing. With this list in place, you can be more organized to make changes to your behaviors because ultimately these are the only things that lead to your results.

Can you see how minimizing the negative ones and increasing the energy put into positive ones will help you achieve your goals faster?

Create a Daily Timeline

The next step is to build out a schedule. Start the schedule with the time you normally wake up and break it down by each hour. Fill in the things that you 100% know you have to do anyway. Maybe you have to get the kids ready for school in the morning. You work from 7-4 during the week. You are part of a volunteer organization our you go to meetup groups on Tuesday nights. To chunk down and avoid overwhelm, what I want you to do is create a daily schedule for tomorrow and tomorrow alone. Now, add the most important thing (Your Now Step) as the thing to do the very first thing in the morning. If this is not practical for you, such as if you have to get to work at five in the morning and the gym doesn't open until six, place your now step directly after you get out of work and make your morning Now Step to put the gym clothes in the car. The reason I mention right after work or first thing in the morning is because it's right after a major task ends. It's a clear transitional period of your day. I've personally found these are the easiest times of the day to make significant changes to your habits. If I finished work, started watching TV, and then said I wanted to write my book – I often got caught up in the comfort of my daily routine and it never gets done. On the flip side, when I wake up, grab my laptop, find a coffee shop in the city I'm in and start writing – I always get the most important thing done first. When you start falling back into your routines, it's easy for this priority to slip away.

Clearly mark off 15 minutes, and only 15 minutes to work on that thing. The reason I choose 15 minutes is because it is short enough of a timeframe for you to not feel overwhelmed and I find that most people have trouble starting something. When they start, momentum takes over from there. 15 minutes could easily turn into 3 hours of productivity. Set an alarm on your phone to go off at the time this begins. As soon as that trigger happens, begin executing. Immediately. Clear all distractions (silence your phone and close all tabs of social media) and then utilize this time to channel all of your focus, concentration, and energy into that one thing. When you move forward with this, you'll clearly have an organized timeframe to take that one action you need to take as it fits into the schedule for the rest of your day. If you're just getting started with this, one task is enough to not overwhelm you. But when people start to build out momentum with their goals, they begin to create a more detailed daily schedule. If you don't add time to the mix, things tend to get pushed to the wayside and you begin to wander off course.

How Habits Are Designed to Function

Imagine for a moment that you open up the calculator function on your phone. When you press the buttons 2 + 2 and then =, what happens on the other side? The number 4 appears on your screen. Habits work very similarly in your mind. Once something happens in the neural pathways of your brain, your body automatically executes on that function and it leads to a specific behavior. In NLP, we call these Strategies. For example, you see a purse at the mall you like, you check if you have $300 in your bank account, you buy it. If you see the purse but your bank account is low, you don't buy it. Unless you have a credit card on hand or you have someone else buy it for you. All joking aside, there are algorithms like this built into your unconscious awareness and these things drive much of your behavior. An algorithm with certain variables is programmed into your brain and when the mental processes run through their course, the actions happen on their own. The solution to change your behaviors is to have a better understanding of how these algorithms function. You can re-write the programming similar to how someone can hack the computer code of a calculator and make 2 + 2 = 5. So when a bad habit is triggered, hacking your mind will automatically and effortlessly have this lead to more positive behavior.

Once you understand how this works and how this functions in your brain, it's simply a programming equation to optimize each habit for the better. So for the remainder of this chapter, forget the content of the bad habits themselves and pay more attention to the structural programming in your mind that goes on behind the scenes of each behavior.

The psychology behind this is simple. Habits are built stronger by repetition. The new neural pathways are created in your brain the moment you take the first action on something. This is the equivalent of carving a line in the sand with the goal to get some water running through it. The next time you take this action, the line is carved deeper, all the way until it's turning into a river in the ground. When you take an action long enough, the neural pathways in your brain are comparable to something as strong and deep as The Grand Canyon, timeless in nature and the habits will effortlessly flow for decades to come.

On the flip side of that are the neural pathways that already exist in your mind for the negative behaviors you are taking. For the most part, these neural pathways have been carved into the sand for many years and they are deep. So they are already a part of your routine. Now, how do we begin to rewire your brain to naturally fire signals down the correct pathways and lead to a more positive action? The better question is also how do we collapse the inefficient ones so those bad habits go away once and for all? The answer is in the letter V. I'll tell you about that in a second, but first, let me explain to you how habits work.

The Habit Loop
1. The Trigger Event,
2. The Action, and
3. The Positive Reward

If you've ever seen the blockbuster movie The Wolf of Wall Street, Jordan Belfort's father, "Mad Max" had a hair-trigger temper. There was one scene where he was sitting on the couch with his wife watching a television show and the phone begins to ring. One of those old 1980's type of telephones where it rang and he had to walk across the room to answer it. As soon as the phone rang, his temper was triggered and he began cursing/screaming about somebody calling his house on a Tuesday night. In this scene, the ringing telephone served as the trigger and the behavior was his anger being unleashed into the atmosphere around him. What was the positive reward? So, let's get back to the letter V and visualize how this works for you. At the bottom of the V is the trigger event. This is the thing in your surroundings that acts as the signal for the neuron to fire down the pathway. Because energy enters our brain through our senses from the external environment, it could be triggered by any one of our sensory cues:

- You **see** a bag of potato chips when you walk in the kitchen.
- You **smell** pizza when you walk by a restaurant for lunch.
- You **feel** a craving for sweet treats.
- You **hear** someone talk about this new dish at your favorite restaurant.
- You **touch** the candy bar in your desk when you are at work.
- It could even be **a thought** in your mind that triggers the craving.

So let's say one of these triggers is represented by a dot at the bottom of the V. If you follow the V up and to the right, the line represents the action you take. If you crave something fatty and salty after the trigger event happens, you might eat an entire bag of potato chips until you reach the top right of the V and get your positive reward of the fatty salty satisfaction. The right half of the V represents a neural pathway of the bad habit in your brain. As soon as the trigger happens, a neuron is fired until you reach the positive reward at the end. At the most basic level, you can go back to the list of negative actions you take during the day and begin to write down the Trigger Event for each one of those habits.

Think of each of these sensory cues as a doorway to your brain. Your brain won't get stimulated by information unless it goes into your body through one of these doors. When you know which door the trigger goes in, this can provide you with the intelligence to make a change to it and do something about it. If the trigger event is reaching in your desk at work and **feeling** the candy bar, you know which door to begin working with. Remove the candy bars from your desk at work and the trigger can disappear. This might lead the cravings to come back in other forms (more advanced motivational psychology), but it's one way to start working on improving your habits - setting up an environment where the triggers are not there. Create a list of all your bad actions and triggers for them.

Building New Neural Pathways

Now, with the understanding of what the Trigger Event is, we can begin to build out a more positive habit when that trigger event occurs. This is done by carving out another neural pathway in your brain. This is represented by the left side of the V. Instead of the trigger at the bottom leading you up and to the right, you can start carving out a groove in the sand so the neurons can fire through a more positive action up and to the left.

As I'm traveling through South America, there's a farmer's market Sunday mornings near me. At this farmer's market is a booth that sells delicious Peruvian potato chips, deep-fried in oil. These things are delicious because of the fatty flavors (from the oil) and the salty flavors from the added salt. My taste buds crave this positive reward! The problem is that soaking things in deep fried oil and adding this much salt is not good for my health. The trigger event is that when I wake up in the morning and I say to myself "It's Sunday", I walk down to the farmer's market and buy 6 or 7 bags of chips for the week. Two days later, the chips are gone.

Another booth is owned by this Venezuelan man and his wife. He sells healthier foods that fulfil the same types of cravings. One of the options he has are sunflower seeds that are roasted with dried olive pieces in the mix. The sunflower seeds satisfy my Positive Reward (the fatty craving) and the dried olives satisfy a saltier and fatty flavor mix. All of this maintains my satisfaction of my positive reward without having to eat something that is deep friend in oil. So if you imagine the V, when I wake up and crave the fatty salty flavors, the neural pathway was taking my body to get chips for my positive reward. But when I can fulfill the same positive reward with the new pathway created (the left side of the V), I now have two pathways that are there. Obviously the first one would be stronger because it's been there for years, but it all starts with carving that first groove in the sand. Actions build habits. So start taking them.

The important thing is to understand that the trigger event will happen anyway (unless you make environmental changes to remove it). The positive reward is something specific you crave. Find out what that is and write that in your planner as well. And then discover a more positive habit that you can go through which is aligned with your goals. At this stage of the game, when you begin to take these actions (perhaps using the $100 check method and other strategies you've learned in this book), you can begin to create these pathways so they are small grooves in the sand. Repetition of a habit builds it up over time.

Building a Dam in the River

Now, as things are, you have two pathways in your brain. Think of this as a river that branches off in two directions. If you're floating down the stream and the canoe goes to the right, this leads to the negative outcome (overweight, not making enough money, being lonely, etc.). Since your mental programming leads to your actions and your actions lead to your results, the very first step to make the change is to start building a dam that prevents you from entering that neural pathway to the right. You see this with classic dog or human training. Many people slap a dog with a rolled up newspaper as soon as he or she jumps on the couch or does something they aren't supposed to do. The immediate pain associated with the bad action starts filling that neural pathway with the perception of pain. After enough repetition, the neurology of that pathway is filled with so much pain, the body is trained to avoid entering it again. When I was a kid, I used to do a bunch of things I shouldn't do in the house. Maybe I ate all the candy from the table or something worse. I forget what it was, but I remember when it was bad enough, my mom would have this wooden spoon in the kitchen and lightly hit me with it. Not hard enough to be abusive, but enough to make me feel the immediate pain from when I got caught in the act. I would have to sit in time out for 10 minutes right after I did this.

Before that happened, the trigger was when I saw the candy. The neuron was fired down the pathway as I started eating it and I got my immediate positive reward of the delicious taste in my mouth. But now, instead of the positive reward waiting for me on the other side of eating the candy, I felt the pain of the wooden spoon and me sitting in time out for 10 minutes when I wanted to watch cartoons. After long enough, even the perception of the pain stopped me from doing this, even when the wooden spoon wasn't there. In the past, the bad habit led to positive pleasure. But now it leads to immediate pain. This is part of the way to reprogram the neurology of your brain to start building up a dam so you no longer go down that bad pathway anymore.

As I float down the river, I see all the danger and caution signs of the dangerous waterfall to the right. When I immediately punish myself for the bad actions, the dam is being built that prevents me from going down that fork in the road again. I naturally begin to float left. In my brain, the trigger event happens, the neuron sees the caution signs and remembers that if it goes down the wrong neural pathway, it is filled with pain. So the positive action should be taken more and more so it starts carving out the groove in the sand deeper and deeper. When you do this long enough, it naturally fires things in the right direction. When this pathway is bigger and stronger than the old one, this is when new habits take over and begin to stick.

The Pattern Interrupt

It's a common thing to find ourselves slipping up. This is a normal part of the optimization process so don't fret. It takes time and repetition to get things 100% right. Focus on making slow and steady changes that are built to last over time. It's not a game of 30 days to change your life. Those programs are built by marketers to sell you a book or a course. It's a game of patience in the form of creating full long-term and sustainable life transitions that stick.

Do you ever find yourself 25% of the way into doing something and then saying to yourself "I shouldn't be doing this."? The bag of potato chips is almost gone. What do you do in those instances where catch yourself beginning to slip? Do you continue until the end or do you make a conscious effort to stop what you're doing and cut the pattern short? In many of these instances, we don't have the external accountability to bring us immediate pain when we're caught in the act. We find ourselves doing something and get caught up in our routines. In this instance it's a good thing to start carving out an Exit Ramp from the bad pathway, leading directly into the good one you are creating. You begin floating down the stream, you notice you went in the wrong direction, and **this conscious awareness <u>is the trigger</u>** to begin floating down the exit ramp immediately back to the positive action. Can you see how we created a trigger within the habit itself? The moment you notice you're on the wrong course, you have to immediately change your course. You put the bag of potato chips away and you finish up by eating nuts or a fruit/vegetable instead. Whatever fulfills your positive reward. For me, the chips are away from me and the sunflower seeds are opened instead.

During my NLP training, I learned a thing called a Pattern Interrupt. When we begin working with a client and they start to have negative thought processes come up and they start talking more and more in a depressive state about the problem in their life, we were taught to sit up in our seats noticeably, sniff in through our nose, and curiously ask "Do you smell popcorn?". The client will try really hard to and get confused when they don't. This interrupts the pattern so we can go back and start leading them down a new path.

The neural pathways in your brain are a blueprint for your actual behavior. When a neuron is fired down one direction, your body immediately goes down that task in the real world. When you close that one off, install a pattern interrupt as an exit ramp to bring you to the positive one, and when you associate immediate pain with the negative action, this is how you have all roads leading in the right direction. Reward yourself immediately after doing good things and the more you carve out this groove in the sand, the quicker it turns to a stream, then into a river, and then into The Grand Canyon.

When you have positive habits long enough, this is when they are no longer considered habits and are simply a part of your lifestyle. They become a natural way of being. I taught you the tools and the structure in this chapter, with one example of the sunflower seeds instead of the chips. Now what I want you to do is take these tools and apply it to yourself. Identify your Exclusionary Behaviors, The Triggers, and the Positive Rewards. Setup the Dams, The Painful Punishments, and the Exit Ramps to lead you to good habits that stick. The Deconstructing Motivation Planner & Journal has clear pages so you can organize your thoughts. You can write down your behaviors, trigger events, positive rewards, and have a more step-by-step guide on how to overcome bad habits.

Get the Deconstructing Motivation Planner & Journal at:

www.DeconstructingMotivation.com

Chapter 10

Mental Programming

SOURCE CODE: BUILDING ALGORITHMS FOR ENHANCED HUMAN BEHAVIOR

Accessing "The Other 90%" of the Human Mind

When many people try to push through habits with conscious effort, they face a lot of resistance, struggle, and have to use a lot of willpower. On the flip side, when you create a change in the unconscious mind, you create an instant change in human behavior. By traditional teachings, they say we can only access 10% of our mind. By utilizing the techniques within this chapter, we can now have full access to the part of our mind which is directly responsible for influencing behavior. Behind the surface-level of your actions, there is an algorithm for human behavior. Think of this like a computer program.

Computers have two types of software:

1. The type that's already installed, and
2. The type you install after-the-fact.

Programming We're All Born With

When you go to the store and purchase a new computer, it comes with pre-installed software to make it function the way it does. This computer code determines how the computer functions at the most basic level. The computer can turn on and off, you adjust the brightness, volume, etc. In human terms, the most fundamental functioning of our program is how we breathe, how we sleep, how we digest, how we are programmed to reproduce, stay out of harm's way, and how the systems function in the human body. The most basic functioning that is pre-built into our DNA and keeps us alive. You learned about this in a previous chapter.

Faulty Programing Installed Over the Years

Secondary to that, is the programming that is built up over the years. Many weeks ago, I experienced my first earthquake while living within the ring of fire. The windows started rattling, the door started shaking, things were falling off my table, and a few seconds later, the entire room shook. Fortunately for me, there was no major damage, but up in the northern part of the country was the epicenter of the earthquake. Buildings toppled, homes destroyed, and people lost their lives. Now, when a truck drives by the house and I feel even the slightest rattle in the windows of my bedroom at night; my heart begins to beat fast. I think it's coming and my body goes into full-alert mode. Significant emotional events happen to us in our lives and our body writes a program based on the experiences of this program. Habits are formed. Knee-jerk responses are created. So when you understand the fundamental structure of human behavior, you can now have a deeper-level understanding of why you behave the way you do, and you'll have the empowerment, tools, and resources to re-write the programming to suit your needs.

The Programming of the Human Body

In NLP, I was trained in a thing called Timeline Therapy. Inside your unconscious mind is a perfect recollection of every experience that has ever happened to you in your entire life. While working with clients, I've guided them back to scenes from 3 or 4 years old and they remembered the scene in vivid detail. One woman I worked with was in her mid-40's and has been suffering from sleep issues most of her life. No matter what she tried or did, she could not fall asleep at a decent hour. During our session, I told her to imagine floating up above her body and looking down at herself, imagining herself on a timeline that stored all of her past (and the perception of future) memories. I instructed her to visualize floating backwards on this timeline to the very first event in her life that caused these sleep problems. It's important not to think of it, but instead to allow whatever visual scene come to her consciousness. She was 4 years old and as she's lying in bed one night, her mom comes in the room and yells at her to go to sleep. Immediately, she crossed her arms and said "No! I go to sleep when I want!". In that one instance in time, outside of her conscious awareness, her behavior was programmed forever. Something as simple as her mom ordering her to go to sleep and her response in that moment can plant the seed for many limiting beliefs, habits, patterns, and behaviors in our lives.

Here is the real kicker...

Once a belief and consequent behavior is formed, we do everything in our mind to re-enforce that belief. Any person trying to attack the belief, will result in you digging your heels in deeper and it will make the belief stronger (replace word belief for behavior). So once the seed is planted, the roots grow, the trunk of the tree gets bigger and bigger and bigger. All the way to the point where it's so large you can't knock it down.

But what would happen if you can go back in time and reset your programming to the emotional state you were in before the seed was ever planted.

This leads me to the next rule of the unconscious mind. Behind every behavior serves a positive intent (reinforcement is the psychology term for this). Whether it's compulsive eating, anger, a shopping addiction, a video game addiction, or procrastination; the behavior may be limiting for our current goals. But there was a time in the past where the behavior served a positive purpose. Once we can find out what that positive purpose is, we can preserve the existing benefits from the limiting behavior. Once we extract those, we can find a new way to maintain those same existing benefits with a more empowering and positive one. This makes that bad habit no longer necessary and we can do the work to release it.

Through Neuro-Linguistic Programming (NLP), hypnosis, and traditional psychotherapy techniques, there are powerful tools to work through these problems in a rather quick period of time. While my sleep client floated above the visual scene on her timeline, she learned that she can make autonomous decisions. That was the lesson she learned from that experience. Just like if I do a complete backup of my computer on May 1st and save all the files... If a virus gets installed on my computer on May 2nd; I can always reset that backup to the time before the virus was installed - eliminating the problem altogether. Our body makes this backup in every moment of our lives.

Through The Timeline Release Technique, I had my client float back to a few days before this problem ever existed. Then I had her float into her body and look through her own eyes, seeing, hearing, and feeling as if she is in that time right now. I do this until she is 100% in the emotional state of pretending it's that time before the event right now. While she is in that emotional state, I ask where that problem is now, is it gone? In 99% of the clients I work with, the answer is yes. If not, we work through other things connected to it. She floats up on her timeline and supercharges the entire timeline between then and now with the new behaviors, positive insights, and positive lessons learned from this session and the experience. When she came back to the present moment, she felt the problem was gone.

I've used this technique on myself for years, as well as with hundreds of other people on many things. I helped people quit smoking, overcome gambling addictions, stop compulsive eating/spending, improve their confidence, and other things that limit them from living the life they want to live. While the surface-level problem is always different, the understanding of the structure about how their unconscious mind stores memories is exactly the same.

- Choose a problem,
- Float up on timeline,
- Float back in time above event,
- Extract the necessary information and insights,
- Float to a time before the event and float into your body,
- Hold the emotional state of the time before the event (reset the program),
- Float back up and install positive emotions, behaviors, and insights in first event,
- Do the same for all of the timeline and all related events between it.
- Come back to the present moment

Can you see that regardless of the specific content of the problem my clients have faced, the structure is always the same? This is the type of thing you really should be learning if you want to understand human behavior. Not only for motivating yourself and overcoming bad habits. But also for taking more control of your emotions and becoming more influential in your communication with others.

I have an online self-study video course that offers a certification as an NLP Practitioner. The course is available for you at www.EvolutionLimitless.com/NLP

There are a few reasons why this works. The unconscious mind can't tell the difference between real and imagined events. There was a University of Chicago basketball study that measured the progress of three groups shooting basketballs into the basket. All three groups had their performance measured on day 1. For 30 days, Group 1 physically practiced every day. Group 2 only visualized practicing, but with no physical practice. Group 3 did nothing. Group 3 showed no improvement. But the interesting fact is that while Group 1 improved by 24%, group 2 showed an improvement of 23% by visualizing alone.

While it takes repetition for a new habit to be solidified, utilizing the structure of your mind with these visuals and symbols; you can follow this visualization processes to do much of the change work for you. The pictures you see in your mind connected to the emotions attached to them are "The Other 90% of the Human Mind", which many people growing up said we can't access. This is it, and that's how we access it. When you learn how to do the right movement of pictures in your mind, it's the same as building a habit by action on the outside.

The next thing to learn is that in the unconscious mind, time is not real. When you want to make a change, it's like the flip of a switch. In another chapter of this book, I mention that the conscious mind is the guard to the unconscious. It prevents influence from coming in and making changes because all of our behaviors that keep us safe and alive are stored in here. But when you understand how to safely make these changes, the changes happen in an instant. Using conscious effort, they say it takes 21 days to break a habit. For me, my first introduction to this knowledge was during my first NLP Certification course back in 2014. For years on end, I would have an addiction to fast food bacon cheeseburgers. No matter how much I tried, I couldn't give them up. During my training, the instructor told me to bring up a picture of the burger in my mind. Then, he asked me a series of questions:

- Is that picture in my imagination black and white or color?
- Near or Far?
- Large or small?
- Where specifically is it in my field of vision?
- Dark or bright?

- Do I see myself in the picture or am I looking through my own eyes?
- Where are the feelings, specifically, in my body as I think of how much I like that food?
- From 0-10, how intense are those feelings?

Just as the unconscious mind stores memories in relation to time on the timeline, accessed by visualization; we also store atemporal memories (memories that are not in relation to time). The finer details of how the pictures in our mind are stored...is how the memory is stored in our unconscious mind. Whether it's a thought of you lacking confidence, being lazy, gambling like crazy, or whatever it is; the structure of how we store memories and the finer details of the picture (bullet points above) are what we can work with.

For anyone who reads this, odds are the picture of the food you like is big, bright, in front of you, you're looking through your own eyes, and colorful. I felt the emotions in my taste buds an 8 out of 10.

The second part of the process was to think of a food that absolutely disgusted me. I saw green nose buggers dripping down the seat on the school bus as a kid. I elicited the fine details of that picture too. That picture was black and white, dark, I saw myself in the picture, and it was about 3 feet in front of me to the left. The feeling was the gag reflex, right in the center of my chest at the bottom of the rib cage with a 10/10 intensity.

When I took the original picture of the fast food bacon cheeseburger up in my mind again, I kept the content of the picture, but only changed the finer details to be the exact same as the food that disgusts me. I drained the color out of it, made it dark, floated out of my body so I saw myself in the picture, moved myself and the burger to the left a few feet in front of me, and I moved the feelings from my taste buds to the same location as the gag reflex. And like the sound Tupperware makes when I close it, I imagined that popping sound to lock it in place.

In that moment, the literal thought of the fast food

bacon cheeseburger automatically gave me the same physiological reaction as the gag reflex from the thought of eating wet gooey buggers.

No 21 days to change a habit. No willpower required. The programming of the human body/mind has a structure to it, and when you make a change in the unconscious mind, change happens in an instant. For years on end after I gave up my fast food burger addiction, I trained myself to be one of the top NLP Practitioners and Trainers in the entire world. I also created my training course to help others learn the same things that have made such a positive impact on my life.

In the upcoming chapters of this book, I'll share with you more advanced NLP strategies that makes sure all of your actions, behaviors, beliefs, and unconscious mental processes are aligned with your goal; from the inside out.

Chapter 11

The Filters in Your Mind

INDIVIDUAL FILTERS OF BEHAVIOR

In Deconstructing Motivation, I talk a lot about the universal drivers of human behavior. These are the natural programming mechanisms in our body designed to keep us alive. Simply by having the knowledge that these exist, this gives you a newfound power to work within the existing motivational systems instead of blindly trying to go against them. Imagine how much easier it would be if you went with the flow of the current down river instead of trying to paddle against the way you're naturally intended to behave. But closer to the surface, there are individual drivers of behavior. Think of these as filters in your mind that are unique to you.

In previous chapters of this book, I said that we are motivated to move away from pain and towards pleasure. While this is true for everybody, one person may be more motivated by pain while the other may be more motivated to move towards pleasure. This is the difference between saying "I want to be in a happy relationship with a person who truly loves me" vs. "I don't want to be single and alone". "I don't want to be broke." vs. "I want to be financially abundant". While this is a very subtle distinction in your language, this could help open up the awareness if the $100 check method of painful drivers are the better option for you or if you're more open to rewarding yourself along the way. In this chapter, I'm going to outline many of these drivers. It'll be your task to understand where you fall on the spectrum and set up a system that works for you. This is another way to make effortless motivation a breeze.

Perfectionist vs. Everything is Fixable

In the online marketing community, there is the philosophy of trying a lot of things, failing fast, getting as much feedback as possible in a short period of time, and then adjusting until things are optimized and you finally get it right. A perfectionist would never get things out in sufficient time to get the data they need to drive effective marketing results. It's common knowledge from all successful individuals that you're going to fail a thousand times before you get things right. Before working through my fears, I used to be a perfectionist. I wanted to tweak every single color on my website, I wanted to get in the perfect shape before I attempted to attract a relationship, I wanted to know the exact details of the fitness plan to follow before I even started. Many times, I actually started taking action. I wrote a book that had close to 400,000 words one year. But I wasn't completely happy with it, so to this date (4 years after-the-fact), it's still not published. Whereas my first published book, I am Not a Millionaire - Making the Shift from Failure to Financial Freedom was written with minimal editing done. I exchanged a number of emails back and forth with an aspiring first-time entrepreneur, copy and pasted them into a word document, and self-published the book a few weeks later. I warned in the beginning that I'm not perfect on the spelling and grammar. But I share real life experiences that has the intent to help. To my surprise, when I set these clear expectations, people didn't mind! After getting feedback from my readers, two and a half years later I published the revised and expanded version, which is clearer, more organized, and in more detail than the first. Some of my readers asked me why I even updated it because they loved the original draft! So where I am at now, I am leaning in the direction of Everything is Fixable. In the past, I would lean too far in on direction (Perfectionist) and nothing got done. But now, after many experiences of never getting what I needed to be released into the market, I leaned too far in the other direction and I was sloppy at times. Now, I balanced it back a bit where I lean mostly in Everything is Fixable, but with more careful intent on reading it through a few extra times before publishing. So instead of an either-or type of scenario, think of this as a pendulum where you can be leaning mostly in one direction. Which one are you in? Is this filter serving your needs? How can you make adjustments to help remove this one little clog in your motivational pipeline?

Options vs. Procedures

One of the reasons why I was so motivated during the police academy is because I was going through a structured program. I knew exactly what I needed to do and how I needed to do it. I followed the procedures to the T and I successfully graduated #1 in my class. Whereas within the first few years of entrepreneurship, I didn't have the clear procedures in front of me. I had to figure things out on my own and there were so many variables not in place. I could have benefited a lot at that time by hiring an experienced business coach who has done this before to guide me along the way. Also, take in mind that these filters are also contextual in different areas of your life. When going to the gym, I am an Options type of person. I like to go in, decide which major muscle group I want to work during the day and then I choose the specific workouts to do on the fly. If I were to follow a procedural program or have to commit to a specific schedule of a personal trainer, I would lack desire and I wouldn't even go. So think about how you can apply this to your goals in life. With my marketing campaigns, I can choose hundreds of different advertising methods, but I chose the option to go with YouTube advertising because I know there is a place I can get my programs in front of people who are actively searching for that exact thing. Do you need a specific set of procedures to follow, or are you more motivated to do things on the go where you have multiple options and multiple choices?

Internally vs. Externally Referenced

This is where you get your permission to act. For many years of my life, I would go to new restaurants on my road trips across the country and always ask the employee, "What's the most popular dish on the menu?". In this moment, I was externally referenced because I got my permission to act from someone outside of me. This type of filter served me when I had a person in clear authority above me to provide this guidance for me. Parents raise their children to listen to their elders. Teachers tell the students what to do. Bosses tell employees what they need to do. But when making the shift to entrepreneur, I had to step into my role as a leader. Even though my filter was not aligned for this, I needed a fix. So what's the solution? Did I change the filter? The answer is...no. Not for many years. In 2013-2014 I had a business mastermind group that I told you about and I setup as system where they were the ones who offered this Externally Referenced permission to act for me. So the really important thing with this one is to be completely honest with yourself. Which one are you? For many years I always didn't want to admit I was Externally Referenced because society preaches us to be leaders and there was ego involved. But this didn't work for me until I actually was self-aware of what my actual filter was and utilized it to my advantage.

Sameness vs. Difference

I wrote the majority of this book inside various coffee shops in South America. For a chapter or two, I wrote them from the desk in the bedroom I'm staying in. But the problem is that things got monotonous and I grew bored easily as my productivity and focus went down. At a company I used to work for from 2012-2014, they had a pattern of changing up the desks we sat at every few months. Many people such as myself need a subtle sense of new-ness and variety in order to keep the emotions going and to not get bored in a routine.

But on the flip side of that, there were co-workers I was with who need the sameness and the routine every single time. Once they get comfortable, they can get in the flow of things and they progress. In reference to using this filter at the gym, maybe you're a Sameness type of person and you hit a plateau. What would you do there? Would you continue with something that served you in the past, or would you find a way to either adjust your filter to make things work for you. Break yourself out of the cycle, while also finding a way to keep the Sameness that you like. Filters are not set in stone for life and adjust over time based on life experiences. But the general rule of thumb is that you want to make sure to work within what your existing filter is.

Independent vs. Cooperative

Do you work better as a team player or do you work better in individual settings? If you can see me right now, I'm sitting at an empty table at a Starbucks in Magdalena del Mar in Lima, Peru, I have my headphones in, my hoodie up (partly because it's cold), and then focusing in on my work by myself. If one of my team members for the vegan company calls me, it kills my focus and I'm done with that task for the day. On the flip side, one of the partners in my company thrives off of this team setting. He wants to work in busy areas with people he can talk to, setup a round table in the office where we are all there talking and throwing ideas off of each other. Depending on what we need to get done, this could work for planning sessions. But for me when I'm in work mode - I tend to be alone. Are you more of the type of person who would prefer to go to the gym alone or with a group of people? I prefer to go there by myself.

Reactive vs. Initiative

For my undergraduate degree, I studied Political Science at Stony Brook University in Long Island New York. I procrastinated a lot on my homework, studying, as well as the assignments I had to complete. It wasn't until the night before the paper was due before I even opened the book. I also studied criminal justice for a year and a half. Some police strategies talk about proactive policing where they clean up the graffiti from the neighborhood. They go in and form relationships with the community before problems arise. Other strategies are more reactive where they respond to problems after-the-fact. Similar to this, are you the type of person who reacts and takes actions after something happens? Or more proactive in nature? This can boil down to accountability groups and the $100 check method if the Reactive filter is what works for you. Don't try to go against your filters, but work within the existing ones.

Reflective vs. Active

Another filter in your mind is if you're the type of person who wants to reflect on things before making a decision to act. Or if you're more on the impulsive side and act right away when things come up. In 2014, I attended a business conference where many startup entrepreneurs were there asking more experienced mentors for advice. One of them had an idea for a software program that was commonly used in Brazil but not in the United States. The mentor told him to call the Brazilian company and ask if they could license out their software to him in the United States. Most of the room nodded their head in agreement and was really impressed by such a great idea! The young entrepreneur in the hot seat nodded his head and was thinking about it, saying, "I think I'll do it!" (read: simply reflecting on it). The experienced business mentor grew furious, stormed out of the room, and then came back a few minutes later with a cell phone to his ear. "I have the CEO of (that software company) on the phone, I explained the situation, and he is interested in negotiating a deal with you". He handed the phone to the young entrepreneur in the hot seat. If you are a more reflective type of person, you should really have an objective set of criteria in place to know exactly when it's time to take action.

Task vs. Relationship

In many cultures throughout the world, it is considered rude to start a business meeting without sitting down, talking about each other's lives, families, and forming a relationship with the person before the meeting. As an American businessman, I find this to be outside my norm. Growing up in New York, we were mostly direct and to the point. I would go out there, find out what task I need to do, execute on it, and get things done. I keep my meetings short and to the point so we can be productive. On the flip side, there are people around me who lean on the other side of things. They are less about the tasks they need to accomplish and more about the relationships they form. While there is a plethora of information on how to use this for business or for interpersonal communication skills, the main thing you want to do right now is become self-aware of where you are naturally and utilize this for your motivation.

Small Chunk, Medium Chunk, Big Chunk

We talked about this one before in another chapter. Are you a big picture thinker who has a lot of great ideas and can strategize but find it difficult to get down into the small chunk details? Or do you naturally gravitate towards the details of things and never really chunk it up too high to see the bigger picture? I'm a Big Chunk person myself. For many years of my life, I had to really try hard to get away from my dreams of the future and get down in the Now Step and other details. In business, there are many tasks I don't want to focus on. So we hire outside marketing agencies to do some of the smaller things. We make sure the company as a whole has people who fit each role. Many low-ranking employees of a company fit perfectly in a role for a chunked down task. A friend of mine, Rob was the best salesman at the organization, closing millions of dollars of sales for the company each year. He was a chunked down salesman who focused on his task of closing the sale. Whereas the CEO of the company has the visionary strategy and fits his role of Chunked Up global tasks. There are middle-managers and other senior executives. It's not a matter of being better than another, but simply knowing what your filters are and where you fit best.

So those right there are some additional filters of human behavior. When you understand what yours are, you can use this knowledge to your advantage to remove any major and minor blocks that get in the way of reaching peak performance state. In the next chapter of this book, we'll drive deeper into ways to remove unconscious resistance that might get in the way of effortlessly acting on your goals.

Chapter 12

Internal Alignment

ALL ARROWS POINTING TOWARDS THE GOAL

One of the main tenants of my NLP Practitioner Training are the Neurological Levels of Transformation. The tip of the pyramid is pointing directly at your goal that you set out for yourself. The goals are hovering above the pyramid like a cloud. There are many levels within the pyramid that need to be aligned in order to have all arrows pointing in the right direction towards your one clear and specific destination.

- Identity
- Values (Priorities)
- Beliefs
- Skills & Capabilities
- Actions, Behaviors, and Habits
- Your External Environment.

When all levels are aligned with your goal, you'll feel less internal resistance when doing the things that you need to be doing in order to achieve your goal. But if even one level is out of alignment, then this could be a major roadblock that takes away from serious motivation.

Level 1 - Your External Environment
At the bottom of the pyramid is the Environment you

are in. In personal development circles, they say you are the average of the five people you spend the most time with. I'm sure that if you look at the people who are closest to you in your life, you share similar behaviors, characteristics, and traits as them. Years ago, I was speaking to the leader of one of the largest social justice movements in the world about motivation, and he said "If you want to be motivated to go to the gym, spend time around people who are already going to the gym." The same holds true in business, confidence/attraction, healthy eating, etc. Whether it's the books you read, the media you consume, the people you follow on social channels, the more you program your mind with the information that comes from them, the more you will subconsciously take on those traits yourself. Most of my early adult life, I was taking advice from life-long employees. People I respected my entire life for advice. But the only problem is that their advice led them to their destination of working a 9-5 job in an office their whole life and retirement in their mid-to-late 60's. When I wanted to be a self-employed internet entrepreneur, I was following the wrong advice which led me down a different path I wasn't meant to be walking on. When I want to eat healthier and all of my friends decide to go out to fast food restaurants, can you see how this external influence plays a major role in my motivation?

In addition to the advice you get from people, there is a very subtle psychology behind the environment you place yourself in. This comes from evolutionary psychology. In the wilderness 10,000 years ago, while we were facing the risk of being eaten by large animals, deadly human tribes, and other dangerous predators; it made sense to blend into our immediate surroundings. When we blended into the surroundings, this meant survival for us. The warrior couldn't see us if we blended into the bush. If you're living in that time and you leave one tribe and move into another tribe, you'd be expected to take on the same customs, actions, and belief systems as them. When you assimilate to the tribe you are in, you have access to the safety and security of numbers, food, shelter, fire, and other resources that kept you alive. If you don't assimilate to the new tribe you want to be a part of, you'd be banished to the wilderness and would most likely die. For tens of thousands of years, this survival mechanism was built into our very DNA. It is so powerful; we begin to unconsciously make these changes without even trying for it.

While we live in different times, the same holds true today. The programming we have in the survival mechanisms of our brains don't go away over the course of a couple thousand years. After years of struggling to stay motivated to build my first business, I made the decision to go to a millionaire entrepreneur conference in Scottsdale, Arizona. Up until that point, I was surrounded by friends who were employees at the job I was working at the time. After work and on weekends, they would play video games, watch movies, go out drinking and partying; which allowed no time to build the internet business I wanted to build. Because I spent my time with them, I unconsciously took on those behaviors.

But after going to the millionaire entrepreneur conference and learning that we unconsciously take on the habits of those people we are closest to; I decided to pay close attention to what influences were subconsciously programming my behaviors through my external environment. I eventually moved into an apartment with two other aspiring entrepreneurs. We took on a number of millionaire mentors, threw out all the televisions in our apartment, and stopped playing video games. While, in the past, I would unconsciously gravitate towards the behaviors of my employee friends, I now found myself making sacrifices and leaving the old life behind; paving way for my assimilation into my new tribe. I would say NO to things that were fun in the present moment. Instead, I did what I saw my mentors do; focus on producing content for my business and putting my time and energy into that. Within six months of being in this new environment; all of us built successful businesses of our own. The same outcome held true in many areas of my life. When I spent more time with vegans, I began eating vegan. When I spend more time interested in personal development and spirituality, I attracted more of those people into my life. For the most part, it was largely unconscious and I did it effortlessly.

When I got more interested in spiritualty, quantum physics, and power of the universe teachings, I saw this same lesson through a different lens. They say that beneath our organs, our atoms, and our electrons; we are made up of energy that vibrates at a certain frequency. Do you ever notice how certain frequencies of music place you in a certain emotional state? When you listen to relaxing music, your body aligns with the frequency and gets more relaxed. When you listen to pump-up music at the gym, you feel more energized and motivated. According to this same spiritual philosophy, when I surrounded myself with those millionaire entrepreneurs, the more time I spent around them, the more my particles subconsciously and quantumly began vibrating at their level, and I began turning into them. A very powerful and unconscious way to make changes in your life is to change your environment and who/what you surround yourself with.

The important thing to think about in your life right now is who are the people that have already achieved the goal you set out for yourself. Do you want to spend more time with people who are already in relationships? More time with people who already built successful businesses? Can you make friends with people who have a daily ritual of going to the gym and exercising? Join a hiking group in your local area? Whether it's people who already achieved the goal you set out for (mentors), there are also other people who are in the same position as you who you can walk this journey alongside. They can help with motivation and accountability while mentors help with guidance. And on the flip side, when you spend more time with people who already achieved your goals, some environmental factors that hold you back from achieving your goals will start melting away. It may be hard to let go of the old, but sometimes that's what it takes to get to where you want to be going.

Other things to think about:

- What **physical things** in your environment are not aligned with your goals? Junk food snacks in your kitchen?

- What **information** do you consume through videos, books, and social media? Who should you start following and who should you stop?

- What people in your life are feeding you information that is aligned with a different type of life than what you want to live?

If you could envision a perfect external alignment that is aligned with your goals, what would it look like? Now, look at your current environment. What specific things in your external environment are not aligned with your goals? How can you adjust, remove, or change some of those things to be more aligned?

Level 2 - Actions, Behaviors, and Habits

Ultimately, your actions lead to your results. Everything else on the pyramid plays a supporting role in making the best use of your daily actions, behaviors, and habits. I spent a lot of time writing about this subject so far, but it's always a good reminder to take a look at two different things when it comes to the actions you take.

First and foremost, you followed the Hierarchy of Ideas to chunk up and down the ladder to make a list of the many actions you need to take in order to move forward on the path towards your goals. You've worked with different motivational strategies to start building out repetition of these behaviors so they become habits. And when you build out the habits long enough, they become an unconscious part of your lifestyle. When I was transitioning my eating habits to start eating more Vegan Plant-Based foods, I had to struggle and try at first. Then I began to notice I was gravitating more towards vegan foods naturally, but it wasn't a 100% way of my life. After long enough, with my environment aligned for it and the habits taking over; one day I woke up and realized that I ate completely vegan for three weeks without even trying to. Actions turn into habits and habits turn into lifestyle. Repetition is key, and I want to remind you to pay close attention to what specific actions are the most important to get you closer to your goals. Some actions feel-good and keep you feeling productive, but may not be the most important thing you should do now.

Secondary to the actions you are taking, please take even more consideration into the actions you should stop taking. After editing this book, I decided I wanted to create a Deconstructing Motivation Planner & Journal where it has worksheets that allow you to write down a clear list of actions that you've been doing, but are no longer aligned with your goals. They go through a psychological process to get to the root cause of why those actions are still here, when and where they formed in your past, as well as strategies to slowly chip away at those blocks so those actions are no longer needed and they go away.

I am not a big fan of an all-or-nothing approach. There is a difference between trying to adopt a strict diet from day one and building out an on-ramp to a more sustained long-term lifestyle. Remove the guilt of partaking in actions that are not aligned with your goals. Just like with the Hierarchy of Ideas, you can chunk up and chunk down to one specific action to work on each week, and build out these long-term lifestyle changes over time. The first step is always conscious awareness of what these things are.

These are called your exclusionary behaviors. When I work with coaching clients, I go through a long-term process to identify the exclusionary behaviors that are occupying their time. We get to the root cause of why this behavior is still in place, what purpose it serves, and then we come up with a solution to remove it and replace it with a more empowering behavior that is aligned with their goals. The full extent of this is beyond the scope of a book, but for the general purpose of your behaviors, take a look at the steps you outlined while Chunking Up and Chunking Down. Identify what specific actions you should be taking. On the flip side of that (more importantly), create a separate list of habits and behaviors you should not be doing anymore. From there, you should have a clear understanding of how to be more aligned.

But even that is not enough for full alignment towards your goals. Years ago, a friend of mine put a fake countdown timer at the top of his website. When a person landed on the sales page, it said the 50% off promotion would be gone in 6 minutes and the counter started counting down. This led to a massive increase in sales for his business. The only problem is that the counter reset to six minutes every time somebody loaded the page. Everything above this 2nd level on the pyramid (Actions, Habits, Behaviors) plays a role behind the scenes of influencing the actions you take. I have a Belief that I should always be honest and forthcoming in my promotions, so that belief plays a role on my behavior. When my friend holds a belief that you need to do what you need to do in order to make more sales, can you see how the different beliefs have different impacts on behaviors? Contrary to popular thinking, beliefs are not set in stone and can be changed. We'll get to that in a moment.

Level 3 - Skills & Capabilities

Another thing that plays an impact on your behavior (one level above it on the pyramid) is your Skills & Capabilities. You may not have all the resources available to you in this moment and you certainty don't have all the skills you need right now. But on the flip side, you can take on the mindset that is more empowering to you. You always are able to learn new things (one day you didn't know how to tie your shoe). You have the resourcefulness to go out there and learn new things. You have access to find the resources you need, even if other people have it. With this understanding, you have nothing holding you back from doing what it takes. Now, what specific skill-sets and resources do you need in order to achieve your goals?

One of my professional goals in life is to publish 14 non-fiction books, create a transformational program called The Limitless Transformation that allows people to break free from the life they feel stuck in so they too can live the life of their dreams. I also want to accumulate $23.8 Million in the next ten years so I can put that money to good use and invest in companies that make a positive impact in the world in the realm of health, medical breakthroughs, clean energy, and personal development.

In 2009-2012, I was at a rock bottom in my life with zero business experience, my only job after college was working for minimum wage in fast food, I never wrote anything in my life outside of school, and absolutely ZERO confidence in my ability to do any of that. At the time, with so much darkness in my future, why even try? Someone like me never built up anything like that before. Someone like me was never worthy of someone who loves me unconditionally. People like me didn't eat healthy. I've never done it before. I didn't know how to do it.

Then, over the next decade of my life, I slowly crawled forward on my journey to reach the point where I am today. The skills I had to learn to get to where I am now are things I didn't know how to do, but I developed them over time. In personal development, there is a natural learning curve that has four stages.

- **Stage 1** is that you don't even know that this type of skill exists.

- **Stage 2** is when you know it exists, but you've never done it before.

- **Stage 3** is when you try to learn it, but just like riding a bike, you keep falling down and can maybe get it right a little bit, but you keep messing up.

- **Stage 4 -** But after going through Stage 3 long

enough, you try, you fail, you adjust, you repeat, eventually you start getting it right and it becomes a natural part of your everyday skillset.

I write this section to help you be more empowered. You won't have the skills and resources you need to do the things now, but deep down inside, you have the resourcefulness to make it happen and learn new complex things over time. To move forward even when you're Standing on the Edge of Darkness.

Let's say one of the skills I need to learn for writing this book is to get 50 reviews on each platform I sell it on. I've never done that before, but I would ask myself the questions: Who do I know that has done this before? How can I contact somebody else who has done this before, even if I don't know them? Try, fail, adjust, repeat. So go back to the pathway you drew out for yourself. See the actions you need to take. In the Deconstructing Motivation Planner & Journal, there is a section to match each action up with a skill you need in order to do that. It allows you clearly plan what resources you have, have access to, or can find in order to get there.

Remember back when you didn't know how to tie a shoe? Think about some time 10 years into the future and look back at where you were today and didn't know how to do the new things you learned and are now second nature.

Level 4 - Beliefs

If you believe all salespeople are sleazy, this is a belief that is limiting you from moving forward with the Action of trying to make sales. If you believe all wealthy people are greedy, this is a belief that is limiting you from moving forward with gaining wealth. There's a level of self-judgement that is blocking you (emotionally) from moving forward. If you doubt your ability to do something, you won't even try.

For years of my life, I studied to become a specialist to help people overcome doubts and limiting beliefs. One of the first things I learned is that beliefs are not set in stone.

What you believe to be true is only true in your collection of memories and past experience that reinforce a belief. A long time ago, a seed was planted in your mind. Perhaps your parents told you money doesn't grow on trees. You accepted this to be truth. You saw your parents struggle with money growing up. You took part-time jobs that didn't pay enough. The bills piled up and all the events in your life built upon this seed like a snowball rolling down the hill. But what if a different seed was originally planted? No difference in the world we live in, but simply a different belief system in your mind. Would it potentially impact your behavior differently? I told you the example of my friend with the countdown timer. I could have been instilled with that belief a long time ago and my actions would have been different. It's no difference in our abilities, but simply a seed that was once planted in our mind.

Somewhere out there is another person who was installed with the belief that the more value you give to the world, the more money you make. Instead of training to make sandwiches, they studied to become a doctor because their belief system told them that being a doctor is a way to make more money. But what if two doctors with identical training and skill-sets graduate from medical school and go out into the world. One believes that specializing in one area will allow him to make more than double most doctors, so he becomes a heart surgeon and his belief leads him to a $400,000 per year salary. The other one has a belief that his time and skills are limited so he also studies business and opens up a clinic that employs a dozen doctors and sees thousands more patients. He earns a net income of $1.5 million per year. Different belief systems lead to different results. Skills, training, abilities, and experiences are all the same.

Years ago, you were installed with many faulty belief systems that were not true, but seem true in your reality today. Such as saying you're not good enough. Or calling yourself a procrastinator. In NLP, there are two separate visualization processes that help you overcome limiting beliefs and doubt. This allows you to access your unconscious mind, go back in time, and overcome many of the limiting beliefs and doubts that are not aligned with your goals and visions of the future. The full extent of the work is beyond the scope of a book. But in general, hold true that beliefs are not set in stone and if you have thoughts and beliefs that are not aligned with your goals - write down on a piece of paper why those beliefs used to serve you in the past, what positive intent they have for you, and why they are holding you back with your current goals now. And then start writing down a list of more empowering beliefs that would serve you better.

"While there are sleazy salespeople out there who rip people off, there are many people in the world that need my product and if I become better at communicating the benefits of this, they will be happy when they buy it. With a money-back guarantee, there is no downside for them." is a perfect example of an empowering belief of a person who once thought selling is bad.

"While I believe that it was hard to stick with diets before, I have a new motivation in my life that is pulling me to make slow and incremental changes that will pay off in the long term" is a better example of someone who believes you have to go on an all-or-nothing diet.

Level 5 – NLP Values & Life Priorities

What's important to you in your life? I've done coaching for many aspiring entrepreneurs to help them break free from their jobs by building a side business which eventually earns them more than their day job; so they can quit, be free, and grow a business of their own. One of my clients was working a stressful investment banking job in NYC that drained the life out of him. He had a good amount of money saved up, was single, the lease to his apartment was ending in 3 months, and he didn't have any major responsibilities. His priorities were aligned with focusing on his business first and foremost.

Another client of mine worked a similarly-stressful job, earning six-figures, and wanted to break free from that to have his own business. But he had a wife, mortgage, and a kid on the way. Do you think my same guidance of quitting the job and spending all of your free time on your business was the same message for both of those clients? Definitely not.

We all have priorities and things that are important to us in our lives. Career/Income, Health, Fitness, Relationships, Spirituality, Family, Hobbies, Experiences. When we rank our top five priorities, as they truly are, this makes room for seeing how aligned we are with our goals. We can also see how we can balance our life to make sure our deepest priorities are getting fulfilled.

You do this by asking the following question: If I could only fulfill one of these, leaving the rest out, which one is the most important to me in my life right now? Rank your top five.

1. Career/Income,
2. Health,
3. Fitness,
4. Relationships,
5. Spirituality,
6. Family,
7. Hobbies,
8. Experiences, or
9. (Insert another life priority here)

For a few years, I always had the stated goal of growing my business, but the thing that was more important to me in my life at the time was working on my fitness and health. I would wake up first thing in the morning and climb a mountain every day to get in shape and business would come around 11 a.m. Then around 4-5 p.m., I would take a break from business and go for a late afternoon bike ride. After losing 70 pounds this way, something inside of me shifted and my business became a higher priority. But between the hours of 11 a.m. and 4 p.m., I scheduled that time to be focused on my business. Many people neglect their stated goals altogether when they are not listed as a top priority in their NLP Values Criteria.

How can you schedule your day to make sure your top priorities are fulfilled on a regular basis, while also making the appropriate room in the day for fulfilling the priority for your stated goal?

Level 6 - Identity

Are you a U.S. Citizen? Are you German? Peruvian? Or Chinese? Are you an entrepreneur? Are you a vegan? Are you a democrat or republican? You see, at the deepest level of our behavior, we have a self-image that in NLP we call our Identity. I have always enjoyed the taste of fried chicken my whole life and my taste buds still crave them when they are dipped in honey mustard. Even when I tried to go on diets, I would still eat them. I never Identified myself as a healthy person, so I acted congruent with this identity. But I am a vegan now so I do not eat meat. That's my identity and this is the top of the pyramid. Do you identify as a procrastinator? Do you identify as being lazy? Do you identify as a healthy person? Do you identify as an employee who is trying to quit your job and start your own business? Or do you identify as an entrepreneur who is working a job on the side to provide for yourself while your business grows on its own? Do you see the difference?

Our inner self-image and language around the subject plays a very powerful role on our behavior. So when you bring up that vision in your mind of you already having achieved your goal, see yourself in that picture and pay attention to your identity, your character traits, your behaviors, and everything about you. For most people, they identify as who they were with behaviors from the past and the other negative labels other project onto them. "You're weird." "You're a loser". This builds up the identity in our mind and it's hard to break free from. But the most important thing is that you act congruent with who you identify yourself as at the deepest level. When you take an action that is in contrast with your identity, you will quickly snap back to your identity and continue to participate in limiting behaviors.

There are many techniques I use on myself to work through this, but for now, act as if you are that person you are meant to be. The identity of who you are after you achieved this goal. Act is if you are this person now. If you feel the temptation to eat junk food, say to yourself that "I am a healthy person and this no longer does any good for my body" as you make the decision with your behaviors to immediately eat something that vibes with you better and resonates with you more.

In summary, when your identity, values, beliefs, skills, actions, and environment are aligned with your goals; this removes many of the roadblocks to motivation and success. It took me years of immersion in a wide variety of psychotherapy, NLP, hypnosis, and other related topics to create major transformations in these areas of my being. For many people reading this today, the simplest action steps you can take are to align your external environment and behaviors with your goals. The rest is more advanced work that would take a trained coach or years of experience to fully grasp.

Make sure all arrows are aligned and pointing up towards your goal at the top:

- Identity
- Values (Priorities)
- Beliefs
- Skills & Capabilities
- Actions, Behaviors, and Habits
- Your External Environment.

Chapter 13

Recharge Your Batteries

AVOID BURNOUT & PRIME YOUR ENERGY
LEVELS FOR OPTIMAL PERFORMANCE

Years ago, I remember reading an article about Mark Zuckerberg, the Billionaire founder of Facebook. They said he wore the same outfit every single day because even the smallest decisions like what to wear in the morning or what to eat for breakfast drained his mental energy away from his most important tasks. He knows the importance of maintaining proper energy levels and utilizing them in the most efficient fashion. On the flip side, do you ever feel like you're simply trying to survive throughout the day, not having enough energy, focus, or concentration to do the things you need to be doing? In this chapter, I would like to talk about some insights I gained over the years to best maintain high levels of energy and use them efficiently.

Each and every morning, we are born to wake up with a 100% charge of our batteries, similar to a cell phone that charges overnight. There are many things we do during the day which drain our batteries. On the flip side of that, there are also things we can do which recharge our batteries throughout the day. You may also experience other benefits from the things I talk about in this chapter. It may help you improve your focus and concentration so the maximum amount of energy is channeled into the proper tasks.

The Morning Success Habit

In the previous chapter of this book, I talk about the neurological levels of transformation. Towards the top of the pyramid are our core values. These are the things that are most important to us in life in this present moment. They shift over time.

During the fall of 2017, I traveled back to Boulder, Colorado with the goal of losing weight. That right there was my highest core value so I made sure the majority of my energy was put towards that first thing in the morning. Immediately upon my arrival in Boulder, I knew what I had to do in order to do it. The National Center for Atmospheric Research (NCAR) and Mount Sanitas had some of the best hiking trails this part of the country has to offer. I built out a habit of waking up first thing in the morning, putting on my hiking shoes, and driving straight to the trailhead. Before my excuses can kick in, before my laziness took over, the simple Now Step I chose to take was simply to drive to the trailhead, get out of my car, and put on my backpack filled with bottles of water.

Notice how you can connect this to The Habit Loop chapter. With this setup of doing the most important task first thing in the morning, there are no "negative" trigger events or habits that get your day off to the wrong start. I set the tone for my day by making this one simple decision. The trigger – First thing upon waking up, I get in my car and drive. My first action was for the thing that mattered the most in the biggest way possible. Also, notice how easy it was to do. I woke up, got in my car, and went for a drive to a specific location. In my mind, I wasn't committing to a strenuous hike through my laziness in the morning. That simply came after because by the time I got to the trailhead, I told myself, "I already came this far, can't turn back now". So instead of viewing the first task as difficult (strenuous workout), it was really easy (simply get in my car and drive). What is one task you can do first thing in the morning?

Waking Up with Energy

I spent years crafting my lifestyle to be able to function fully without the use of an alarm clock in the morning. I also chose places to live without distractions of noisy roommates or city streets to ensure proper rest with uninterrupted sleep in the evening. I woke up every morning with a 100% charge of my batteries. By the time I reached the trailhead, I was ready to go. For anywhere between one and two hours every morning, I made the conscious decision to move my energy from the batteries within me, into the thing that was most important to me at the time. By the time I reached my car after a strenuous hike up and down the mountain, I was functioning at about 60%. Imagine this, not even two hours after I woke up, I already accomplished my most important task of the day. While you may look at this and see 40% of my energy was drained, I see it differently. I finished what was most important to me instead of running out of energy and never committing to it at all.

Comparing this to many years prior, I would often times wake up at 4:30 in the morning to drag myself out of bed, already exhausted. I would then go to a customer service job where I got screamed at by angry customers all day when their cars broke down and the company's warranty didn't cover the repairs. I filled my body up with fast food and sugary drinks. By the time I got out of work by 4 p.m. that day, I was completely drained and exhausted. 95% of my energy levels were depleted and I didn't have it in me to even get myself to the gym. I would go home, pass out on my bed for most of the night, and then do this on repeat. The energy left to put into growing my side business was non-existent. Can you see the importance of paying attention to your energy levels when you want to motivate yourself to do things that are important to you?

Your Starting Energy Levels

The very first thing I want you to think about is what

percentage of batteries do you wake up with every morning? Do you wake up with a 100% charge like I do after I made the conscious decisions to optimize my life for this? Or do you find yourself waking up after many snoozes of the alarm, beginning the day at 58% like I used to do in the past? What could be a potential solution to help you get extra sleep? Work with a stress management or sleep specialist to get better rest during the night. Go to bed at an earlier hour instead of staying up late. Remove environmental distractions that keep waking you up throughout the night. I had one client who suffered from sleep problems all the way up until he quit his job. His job was the root cause of his anxiety and when he shifted careers, his sleep improved perfectly.

Assuming that is taken care of, my best advice is to simply put your focus and attention into opening up the faucet first thing in the morning and let your energy begin to flow into the most important task of the day. Similar to how I put on my shoes, got into my car, and drove to the hiking trail; the faucet was open and the water flowed out from there. I didn't need to muster up motivation to think about the hard task. Once the chain of events started, I went with the flow as the momentum took over and pushed me forward.

Impacts on Energy Levels

Imagine as if you are a ball of light similar to the sun in outer space. You are radiating this energy at your core where everything you do and things around you will begin to suck the energy out of you like miniature black holes in space. What things in your life are the metaphorical representations of black holes to you? The things that subtly drain your energy away. For me, the first ones come in the form of environmental distractions. They say it takes 28 minutes to regain focus when your concentration is broken away from a task. In the early days of starting my current business, with four team members placed in an office, it's easy for "One quick question" to break focus from a task and have energy being sucked in all different directions from there. Instead of channeling my energy into the thing I was doing, it was being pulled away from me into something completely off-point and completely unrelated. If I accidentally leave a social media tab open on my browser, the ding of a new message coming in subtly sucks my energy in that direction. Notifications on my phone do the same thing. So I remove distractions and align my surroundings with things that don't pull me away. Instead, I choose to surround myself with people and things that push back me on task when I go off course. At the gym, the example could be if you work out with somebody who stands around and talks all the time compared to working out with somebody who is a constant reminder of "You are taking too long of a rest, get back on track."

But what about if you are forced to work in an environment that is full of distractions? For me, I separate the tasks I do into different categories. When I want to write a chapter of my book and be in flow state, I lock myself in my room with my laptop and turn off all distractions. But when I'm in work environments surrounded by distractions, I choose different tasks that I can complete with less mental brain power. One example of this would be designing the cover for my book.

Disorganization and Thoughts in Your Mind

I mentioned earlier that Mark Zuckerberg literally wore the same outfit every day because a micro-decision like choosing his clothes in the morning would drain his energy levels. Many people start off the day without a clear schedule or plan of things they need to get done. Number one, this could lead them to be pulled in any which direction where life drags them through the day – instead of being on course and intent on what they need to be doing. You ever have days like that where one thing pulls you off track from the beginning and you never get back on course?

The same holds true with thoughts in your mind. If you're constantly overwhelmed and thinking of all the things you need to do or if you're too far chunked up on the Hierarchy of Ideas, these mental thoughts drain your energy like a hundred apps being open on your phone all at once. If I woke up in the morning and kept being pulled in all different directions about which trail to hike on, that would drain my energy before I even start. I would fall into analysis paralysis and never even do it. But instead, I knew that each morning I would drive to Mount Sanitas, go home to shower, get my laptop and then go to Trident Café for coffee and a work session after that. During that time, I never had a clear plan for what I would do after 1 p.m. so I noticed my afternoons kept getting pulled off track. I might go for a bike ride, walk through the mall, or go out to a restaurant with friends. While I enjoyed my experiences and life was good, when it came to my goals; nothing got done in the evenings. This is a balance that didn't really make a big difference for me at the time. Depending on how motivated you want to be, set your schedule according to plan. There is more to life than simply being productive.

I remember watching one Star Wars movie where some space ship goes through the universe and sucks all the energy out of a sun to power its engines to go on to the next solar system. You could physically see the white light of the sun being sucked in through a hole and into the space ship's energy reserve systems. This is the clear singular direction you want – instead of a hundred black holes subtly draining the sun rays in hundreds of different directions. The more energy you channel into one thing, the more it will build up the power and be great.

Emotional Distractions

Many weeks ago, I set the intent to edit the first five chapters of this book. I placed my phone on my pillow, went over to my desk, and put binaural beats music on to focus. It was a Sunday where my girlfriend went out with her family and I was emotionally calm; ready to put all of my efforts into my book. Three hours went by and the first two chapters were edited to perfection (at least I hope they were for you). I hit a perfect state of concentration and focus. Then, I realized my phone died, I plugged it back in and I got a number of text messages and missed calls from my worried girlfriend. She was concerned because I didn't respond right away and I normally do. I care about her feelings more than anything in the world so feeling her pain and suffering took an emotional toll on me. My productivity went away. Can you see how in this instance, my emotional state had an impact on my motivational levels? To the extreme example, you can't run a marathon when you're hungover from the night before.

The same holds true for other emotional things you have going on in your life. While starting my coaching practice, I put a strong emphasis on emotional balance techniques, meditation, mindfulness, and working through a lot of the stress, anger, frustration, and anxiety that most people face. Many of these emotions can be the fuel that propels you to do many things you do (such as exercising). For many tasks that require creativity, it could take a toll on your mental reserves. You're not operating at peak performance state. When I faced adversity with my first business and I was having medical problems due to an unsafe buildup of stress, months went by with no work being done because all the stress inside of me was like a heavy blanket that kept me weighed down and unable to be productive.

So if you're facing a lot of emotional drainage in your life, there are many tools and resources out there to work through this so it doesn't take a toll on your life. The number one tool that I can't recommend enough is The Emotional Freedom Technique (EFT), which quickly releases unwanted emotions from your body.

Toxic People in Your Life

In spiritual communities, the call these people energy vampires. Many years ago, I used to work with a client named (blank) who was a constant drain on my energy levels. He was always down and depressed on life. No matter how much I tried to cheer him up, get him to see things more positively, he would always have his low energy levels drag me down. I'm sure you have people like this in your life. The things they do, the things they say, and the energy they radiate has an impact on you. I purposely distance myself from people who are energy vampires because I found them to be a constant drain on me.

On the flip side of that, there are people who are energizing and empowering to be around. Something about being with them just lifts you up and recharges you like plugging your cell phone into an outlet when the levels are low. I always like to surround myself with positive people who bring me up as well as people I feel naturally comfortable around. While a lot of the comfort about being around people comes from inner-work I've done on myself in terms of my confidence, some people are a better fit for you than others. We all resonate with different types of people, so there is no one-set way for selecting who these people are. Simply pay attention to if this person energizes you or drains you when you are with them.

The second thing I want to talk about are Past Emotional Traumas. While we all may view the word trauma as something like being assaulted, in a war zone, or car crash; a looser definition of the word encompasses all things that have an emotional impact on us. I've been cheated on by many girlfriends in the past. Even though those events are close to a decade behind me, something about it still lives in my subconscious. Through many techniques I learned through NLP (The Timeline Release Technique), I was able to clear up a lot of this past emotional baggage that I've been carrying around for many years. I don't think anybody can get through all of it (let me know if you do!), but if the things from my past used to bother me at an 8/10 in intensity, it's lingering around a 1 or 1 and a half right now.

Recharge Your Batteries

Similar to how certain people can drag you down or lift you up, there are other things in your life that do the same.

Many introverts feel energy drained when they are around other people or are in busy environments. An old roommate of mine, Boris, would always have his energy levels lifted up and recharged when he went out to the night clubs on weekends after a long week working on his business. It was a reward for him to go out Friday and Saturday night. He often would wake up early the next morning and be more productive and energized than ever before. Me, on the other hand...I always used to feel drained when I am in environments like that. I much prefer a long hike through the mountains, being in nature, and vibe more with a relaxing coffee shop atmosphere with jazz music playing subtly in the backdrop. What does it for you?

Another thing that does wonders for me is the right length of a nap. I mentioned before that I'm an internet entrepreneur and I never use an alarm clock. When I live in Boulder, I would wake up naturally at 6:30 or 7 in the morning to go hiking and work from coffee shops after that. I would recharge my muscles with a large meal for lunch, usually a chipotle vegan bean burrito. Around 1:00 in the afternoon, I would sometimes find myself falling asleep with a 3-to-4-hour power nap. With my most productive work done for my fitness and my business by noon, the nap is what was needed to recharge my batteries for finishing up my day. There are many sleep studies that talk about an ideal length for a power nap based on the brainwave cycle of your sleep. A 20-minute nap can recharge me, while a 40-minute nap places me in a different sleep cycle, so breaking out of that leaves me exhausted.

Think about things you've done in the past that recharge your batteries. What specific things do it for you?

The Foods You Eat

Ever since launching this natural foods company, I noticed a lot of my team members partake in a practice called intermittent fasting. This is where you spend 16 hours per day not eating anything at all. Only water. At 6:00 p.m., they stop. And then their first meal comes at 12:00 noon, right in time for lunch. While they quote many health benefits of this practice, I do it in the mornings for mental clarity and energy. You see, when I eat a big burrito or plate of pasta, my body's natural energy reserves shift away from my brain and towards digestion. The digestion of the food mixed with the size of meals place many people into a food coma.

Years ago, I would always eat a large breakfast, followed by a few cups of sugar-filled coffee to keep me up throughout the morning. For lunch, another large fast food meal followed by more sugar-filled coffee. Instead of a Zen-like state of clean energy flowing at a baseline, my days were filled with overstimulation (peaks from the sugar rush), followed by the crash (food coma and sugar wearing off). I was never in the proper state to get things done. When I eat more natural foods, plant-based meals with no artificial chemicals or preservatives, I align more with that Zen-like flow state the helps me with my writing. I don't have a magical formula for the ideal nutrition and diet, but I simply know what works for me. Think about what things make you crash 30 minutes after you eat or drink them. Think about what meals don't have a big impact on your energy levels. Obviously, the energy and fuel you need as a bodybuilder will be different than if you're and entrepreneur and writer such as myself. What works best for you? Try different things out, don't be afraid to fail, and learn from experience.

Divine Flow State – Beyond Humanly Emotions

In the spring of 2015, I spent virtually all of my waking hours working on my new business. I would wake up early, force myself to work late into the nights, and I was experiencing short-term sprints that got me some results after I ran fast. But over time, this began to take an emotional toll on me and it burned me out. I worked harder, drank lots of energy drinks to keep me moving throughout the day, but the 14-hour days I put in eventually caused me to burnout. Similarly to this, at the gym, bodybuilders who don't give themselves proper rest are subject to physical injuries as well. Musicians might reach a plateau with the music they write or perform with. Your mind might fill up with so many thoughts and it takes away from your performance. Sometimes we need an extended period away from something, both physical and emotionally, to clear our mind and gain clarity in our life. A reset period.

When I wasn't getting the results I wanted from hard work alone, I finally tried to do something different. I decided to take a rest. I got an invitation from an old college friend to take a road trip around the Southwestern United States with me. We drove up from Phoenix to Sedona, Arizona, the Grand Canyon, Las Vegas, where I eventually dropped her off at a friend's house in LA. Then, I continued to unplug from everything even more, no longer having anything business on my mind to the point where I was traveling on a deserted stretch of open highway between San Diego and Yuma, Arizona. With the windows down, Fleetwood Mac – Go Your Own Way blasting in typical cross-country road trip fashion, it's as if all the thoughts and humanly emotions drained out of me and my body was left with an open and empty container.

I was left with a complete and total sense of divine peace, stillness, and relaxation – in a naturally meditative state. A burst of insight came up from within and told me to create a video training course teaching other people how to build internet businesses like I did. The subtle vibe of this energy was different than any other type of emotions I remember experiencing before. It was more inspirational in nature than a regular thought.

I mentioned earlier in this book that there are three parts of the human being:
1. The Conscious Mind.
2. The Unconscious Mind, and
3. The Higher Self

When I turned off all the external noise (conscious awareness), and drained out all the emotions and thoughts from my unconscious realm, it was similar to being at a loud concert and the loud speakers suddenly turned off. Silence filled the atmosphere. I could hear something deep inside that I never tuned into before. In spiritual teachings, they say this is the divine source of energy from the universe that flows through me. For many people in Western society, this energy is tuned out by the everyday noise.

I opened up the channel to this source of energy and let it flow through me. After watching a beautiful sunset from a restaurant in Yuma, Arizona – I was living in a timeless bubble of reality without any sense of time, deadlines, or needs from the real world. I was completely relaxed and at peace. I made my way back to Phoenix later that night and began channeling this energy by morning.

I bought a computer program to edit audio recordings and a microphone to record my voice over PowerPoint slides. I called it The Fundamentals of Entrepreneurship training program. For three days straight, I got the bulk of the work done with this program. I launched an advertisement on one website and made $1,650 in sales in my very first day. With the payment system and website in place, for the next month straight, I had $300, $650, and $700 sales days flow in effortlessly.

In sports, they call this Getting in the Zone. I call it Flow State. It takes turning off the mental switch, releasing humanly emotions, placing yourself in the proper environment to tune in to it, and then opening up the faucet to let the energy flow. Similar to how I wrote this entire chapter in 30 minutes without a break. It's not an emotion in the typical emotional way that you feel. This is the energy that comes from somewhere else. It's this same energy that recharges your body while your conscious awareness is turned off while you sleep. I can't recommend enough the importance of doing personal work on yourself to properly balance your thoughts and emotions and be able to unplug from the traditional way of life for a while, to tap into these things. Maybe not as a daily or weekly behavior, but you'll know when it's the right time once in a while.

Conclusion

In summary, there are a lot of factors that impact your energy levels. You want to imagine that your body is filled with a white light. Everything you do during the day drains some of this energy out of you. Pay close attention to where this energy is being channeled into. Some of the light is gone and it fills up the television when you watch Netflix. Some of it goes into what's important to you. The more you pay close attention to where this energy is going, how to maintain it, and how to recharge it; the higher states of peak performance you will reach.

Success and completing things is not so much about a use of time, but a use of transmitting energy into something. Clear, focused, energy without any emotional, mental, or physical drain is what will help you the most.

What charges your batteries?

What things in your life subtly drain them?

How can you conserve your energy even more?

Chapter 14

Deconstructing Motivation

HOW TO EFFORTLESSLY MOTIVATE YOURSELF TO DO ANYTHING IN LIFE

Pain Sets You in Motion

There's an old story about a man who walks into a convenience store and sees a dog whimpering in pain in the corner. The man asks the clerk "What's wrong with that dog over there?" The clerk tells him that the dog is sitting on a nail. "Why doesn't he get up and move?" the man asks in confusion as to why the dog would continue to lay there. The clerk looks up and says to the man, "I guess it doesn't hurt bad enough yet." When it is freezing cold outside, you seek shelter or at least put on a sweater. When you're starving to death, you do everything in your power to get food. If you're a little bit cold, you can deal with the pain. If you're a little bit hungry, you can wait a little bit longer. Just like the natural drivers of pain moving you to take action, the same holds true with your goals.

There comes a time in your life where you're not satisfied with the where you are right now. That's probably one of the reasons why you picked up this book. You have these goals you set out for yourself, but you've been struggling to fully commit to them. The only problem with where you're at right now, compared to the freezing cold or hunger story is that there is probably a series of safety nets in place that keep you comfortable enough where you are. Perhaps you're working a job you don't like and it's not making you enough money. In the end, it sucks and you're barely getting by. But you're still getting by. You probably have a roof above your head and food in your mouth. All things you should be grateful for. You're feeling the pain but the natural pain threshold is not high enough for you to take action.

In the first chapter of one of my other books, I talk about my experience of being unemployed for many years before building the internet business that led me to my dreams. A headline in that chapter was called Rock Bottom Sets You Free. For many years of my life, I had a hard time getting a job. This left me broke, depressed, and stuck where I was. I suffered from all the things you probably suffer with too. I was dissatisfied where I was, I had no clear direction to work towards, I would try one thing after another and failed all the time. I had my vision of the future but I never even believed it could unfold. My fears kept me paralyzed and stuck in place. I lacked the energy, drive, commitment, or purpose to move forward with anything. I was complacent.

Deep down in my life, I was waiting for somebody to come and save me. Somebody to hand me the magic formula on my lap or perhaps even do the work for me. But there's an old saying in the startup community that opportunity often comes in the form of hard work and overalls. In order to make this change in your life, you're going to have to do it yourself. And the longer you wait, the more painful life will become. Your heart truly knows what's more important to you than anything in this world and follow your heart because when you move in that direction, it's going to come.

Without the knowledge I shared with you in this book, I was stuck in a holding pattern for many years. I just thought

I was an unmotivated person and this was handed to me at birth. I've been called a procrastinator all of my life. The only problem for me at the time was that I believed these lies and I didn't take the time to tap into my Why and find this source of **Limitless Unbreakable Energy**. At the time, this was back in 2011. I read these books on entrepreneurship of people who escaped even worse rock bottoms in their life and went on to build multi-million-dollar businesses and share their experiences to help others do the same. In that moment, I told myself, "I wanted to be someone who does the same." I want to build a successful internet business and help other people who were broke and stuck in life set themselves free. After driving 2,000 miles across the country, I made friends with the authors of one of these books and he told me, "Andrew, if you want to help other people with something, you're going to first have to do it yourself."

So I went on a journey full of pain, struggle, lack of motivation, but in the end I finally did it. I didn't make a million dollars, but I built an internet business that earned me passive income and allowed me to travel all across the country and the world. I called this book I am Not a Millionaire - Making the Shift from Failure to Financial Freedom. The most recent version of that book was released in January 2017. Six years after I set this purpose for myself. With this undying purpose within me, I was willing to face obstacles, failures, struggles, and risks in order to make this happen. During that journey, I found myself virtually homeless and out of money on many occasions. But I also had some of the greatest experiences along the way. For the past five years now, I haven't ever needed to use an alarm clock, I set my own hours, and I have the freedom to go where I want. It's this destination that made the struggle of the tunnel worth it each and every single time. It's worth mentioning that before I had that first "Big Win" in my life, I completely doubted myself and faced all the procrastination one could face.

Traditional advice from parents, teachers, and society tells you to play it safe. To not take risks and they are partially right. But many of the people who I've met on my journey who have accomplished great and wonderful things live by a different set of values and beliefs. They have a mission and purpose in this life that is so strong, that whatever happens between now and their destination is just an acceptable risk they are willing to take. They aren't reckless, but at the same time they take calculated risks. Follow the advice of others who have walked in your shoes before. Not the ones who gave up, but the ones who made it to their destination.

When you have a weak purpose, you're going to easily give up or go off track. But if you remember my story from the police academy chapter, when the purpose is strong enough - you'll go through hell and back and never deviate from the course. Never deviate from the course. There's much debate in the personal development communities whether we have a life purpose or just a series of purposes throughout life. While I feel there may be some truth to the former, for the purpose of motivation – it's indisputable about the necessity to put energy into your current goals.

Also, realize that once we achieve a big goal in life, another will come up. We set a goal for ourselves, we achieve it, and we move on to the next. After I build my internet business and published my book, I moved on to the next goal from there. I reached my financial goals but my health and fitness were suffering. My relationships and social skills were weak. My emotions were way out of whack. Similar to driving across the country and getting mentored by millionaires, I went on those journeys throughout life and published books about them too.

Looking back on this experience, it really puts it all into perspective. Those big goals you set out for yourself in the future are nothing more than small stepping stones that you'll have once walked on through this journey we call life. When you find your Why, and **Set Your Destination**, know that there will be a hundred more destinations after that one. New goals keep coming up. So with this new understanding, why not simply enjoy the process of every step along the way? Many people associate pain and struggle with the things they need to do. But when I lost 50 pounds in three months back in 2016, I never forced myself to do exercises I didn't want to do. I simply went on a hiking trail and walked through beautiful scenery in the mountains. Similar to that, you can find things you enjoy to do along the way.

So with your destination set, you want to make sure that all arrows are pointing in that one clear direction. If you can imagine a destination on a map, most people go wandering lost and aimlessly in any which direction. But what if you write down your very clear and specific goal and frame that up on your wall as something to live by and never go off course? That no matter what you do in life, this is the one clear destination that magnetically pulls you back and gets you back on focus as the one direction to move. I've coached hundreds of first-time entrepreneurs over the years and the problem I see time and time again is that they suffer from Shiny Object Syndrome. They set an ill-defined goal of "Wanting to make money" so they jump from one thing to another when their current idea doesn't work out right away. The largest e-commerce site in the world, Amazon.com was formed back in the 1990's, with no deviation from their path. While the strategies and tactics to get you there will shift and vary, the vision you are building is timeless and is never going to change. Write it down and never go astray.

So, you have this pain you're feeling that is starting to wake up your emotional body and push you in a new direction. Listen to what that is. You are starting to tap into your desires and find your Why and what is important to you. You have this vision you set out for yourself, so now how are you going to get there? That's the million-dollar question. This is where you want to have **The Step-by-Step Path**. To be honest, it's not going to be there. So many people never move forward on their goals because they spend all of their time in planning mode. They want to have the 100% confidence and certainty that the actions they take will lead them to their destination. And they want to know everything that has to be done before they begin. This is unrealistic and it's never going to happen.

Think of things more along the lines of a spiritual sense. In the esoteric future, the destination is waiting for you and you have to blindly take one step with faith that the next is going to unfold itself after this first one is taken. In a more practical sense, you're going to take action on your goals. Some things will work; some things won't work. You'll have to adjust and then even more things will come up and chaos will unfold. The road to your destination is filled with uncertainty and this is something you can get excited about! It's frustrating at first, but eventually you can embrace it as a normal part of the process.

But, at the same time, one of the built-in traits for our biology is the need for certainty. That the energy we use isn't going to be wasted and our actions are being put to good use. So that's where The Hierarchy of Ideas comes in handy. This is the organizational structure of your brain to separate higher-level chunks to the more specific low-level chunks and arriving at your now step. I outlined two examples in this book of how I outlined and planned my book and how someone can create a fitness routine to get in better shape. When you start with your destination and work your way backwards from there, it's like paving the general pathway that will give a clearer sense of direction. All the steps won't be there, but at least it will be enough to eliminate your overwhelm, get organized, and build the confidence to take that first step.

This chapter ended on finding your Now Step. The one specific task that you should channel all of your focus and energy into until it's complete. The analogy I often use is like those water gun games at carnivals. It shoots out a steady stream of high-pressured water that you aim into a bullseye. When you hold the water stream on the bulls-eye, a balloon fills up and your goal is to hold it until it pops. You can't go around shooting multiple streams of water at once. If you have multiple targets you have to hit, get the steady stream of focus into one of them, pop the balloon, and then readjust your focus into the next. But when you're flipping the switch from planning to action mode, this singular focus is what you need to do. I can't stress this enough.

But the problem with many people, even when they go through this process and have their destination, path, and their now step is that they fall into one of the various **Dopamine Traps** that drain their energy away from their most important tasks. A constant string of pings from social media, video games, app games, television, motivational videos, the learning loop and other distractions. Their energy is constantly being drained and sucked away into those other things instead of being properly focused into the stream of water to blow up that first balloon and get it complete. I don't blame them because all of these dopamine traps are carefully constructed to keep you addicted, based on a scientific understanding of your natural drivers of human behavior.

So that is where you began to learn about your **Motivational Drivers**. You're standing at the front of the tunnel with complete focus on your Now Step. The end destination is so far away, so you may or may not feel the magnetic pull from the end. When you Burn the Boats with the $100 check method, you light a blazing fire behind you so all of a sudden the pain you're running away from overpowers the perceived pain of doing the necessary task. Similar to the pizza at the exit of the gym, you can place positive rewards directly on the other side of the Now Step to magnetically pull you through the task to get there. Remember at the end of the chapter where I talked about Maslow's Hierarchy of Needs and you can use these types of natural human drivers to be the things that pull you forward. Find what your body is craving now and place it directly on the other side. Take the action, reorganize yourself and find the most appropriate Now Step to do this again.

This in itself is enough to have the focus, motivation and dedication to keep moving forward towards your goals. If you stopped reading right here, this would have been enough to make this book complete and make reading it be worth it. But this book is called Deconstructing Motivation, so I wanted to include some advanced strategies as well.

In the next chapter of the book, I talked about how to **Overcome Your Fears**. When you're standing in the tunnel and you want to move forward on a task, you might sometimes notice a force field in front of you that prevents you from moving forward. Something inside of you is feeling the blockage and it's holding you back. This all boils down to the pictures in your mind. This is the way your unconscious mind stores thoughts - as pictures and symbols. So when you think of the worst-case fear of what might happen when you take this action, bring up a clear picture in your mind and see yourself in the picture. There should be an emotional charge to it. When you release the self-judgement about who you are in that picture if you fail, this will release the emotional charge enough for you to walk through and step forward on the task. This is done in a client-setting with a series of rapid emotional release techniques. But at the most basic level, you simple want to redefine that picture and paint it in the best possible light. Make it so you're emotionally ok with whatever happens on the other side of that fear (as long as it's not a fear that puts you in harm's way). There is a lot of stuff going on in your mind so use at your own risk. Similar to the fear of failure is the fear of success. The self-judgement you face if you successfully achieve your goal. The process is the same. Redefine the picture in your mind so you're emotionally ok. This opens up the force field for you to walk through and talk to that person you're attracted to, make that sales call, or to work past your embarrassment of going to the gym when you're out of shape. Whatever it is.

After you overcome your fears, you should also have a reasonable expectation of the **Obstacles & Setbacks** you're going to face along the way. The best way I can define this for you is that the journey you're embarking on to build your vision is a methodical optimization process. One of the online training programs I co-created is called The Surefire Sales System. The end destination of this is to help entrepreneurs and salespeople stop relying on the individual sales they want to close. Instead, they should play a game of large numbers and build out a sales system that converts on a consistent basis. So yes, you might blow five sales calls. But you learn that you're attracting the wrong type of customers who may not have any money. You advertise somewhere else and you find the right people who are a right fit for you. But you get scared at the end and never ask for the money. You learn that you should ask for the money, and the next 10 people say no because you didn't properly explain the benefits of your product. You explain the benefits, but people say they will think about it, never to call you back. Then you start to paint a picture of the pain they feel without your solution so their emotional drivers kick in. You add a bit of scarcity - saying the 50% off offer is only valid if they buy right now. You close the sales, but more importantly - you optimized the process. You might have gotten no external sales on the first 100 sales calls. But with this constant optimization, can you see how you removed a lot of the obstacles the prevented people from buying? You can now play the game of numbers and funnel more leads into the system with the predictability of 15 out of 100 sales closing. Focus on the end goal and don't view those things in the beginning as failures at all. It's simply an optimization process. If you're reading this book for something besides business, draw parallels and create your own optimization process. The road to your destination is filled with a million speed bumps, rejections, setbacks, and other things along the way. Before I went on this journey myself, I thought everything was supposed to go right. It's not. Chaos is the name of the game and if you face it, you know you're on the right path. The only failure you can face is if you don't move forward, learn and adjust along the way, and you never optimize the process - which ultimately leaves you never doing anything and you stay in place. If you don't know what to do, hire a coach or mentor who has done it before.

So once you know what to do and have the proper expectations, it all boils down to persistence and consistency of the actions you take. In the **Internal Alignment** chapter, you learned about the neurological levels of transformation and how each one of these levels plays a significant role on your behavior. You subconsciously pick up the traits and characteristics of the external environment you place yourself in. Read the right books, take the right trainings, view the right media, and surround yourself with the right people who are aligned with your goals. Setup your environment to be as close as possible to what life would be like if you had already achieved your goal. Since a characteristic of our behavior is to blend into our surroundings, this is the easiest way to align ourselves completely. Also, remove the negative environmental influences that are not aligned with your goals. Above your environment and behaviors are your skills and capabilities. You may not have the resources available to you right now, but the character trait that suits you best is to have the resourcefulness to know that the world is full of what you need. Find people in your network who can teach you what skills you need. Go outside of your network and meet new people who can teach you the skills you need if you don't know anybody yourself. If you lack the money to build a business but you have the skills, there are many people with the money to make up for the things you lack. Personal trainers at the gym have the resources to help you with your fitness. Above that, are your beliefs. If you doubt yourself, or have conflicting beliefs, this will also impact your behavior. If you think selling is greedy, you can redefine the belief in your mind that it's simply a way of communicating the benefits of a product that provides a solution in a person's life. You are an informational outlet to get that message through to people. You don't have to be a high-pressured salesperson if that's not your personality type. Sometimes the product simply sells itself. Or if you think you have to be in perfect shape before you attract a relationship, this is a limiting belief that will get in the way of going after someone who might want you for your personality. Your NLP values (life priorities) tell you what is important to you in your life right now. List them for what they are and if your goal does not fall into the top category, make sure to schedule your time to make sure you have a well-balanced life and all areas are being fulfilled (money, family, relationships, health, spirituality, growth, experiences, contribution, etc.). Then at the top of the pyramid is your identity. Don't fake it until you make it in the sense of putting up a front. But with the core of who you are, you should truly live it and be the person who lives this vision for yourself every day. Flip the switch in your mind and view yourself as being a healthy person, now. As being a motivated business person, already. Who is a great boyfriend or girlfriend, today. Bring up a picture of who you are after you achieved your goal. Take a clear look at this picture in your mind and pay attention to the character traits. Start being this person today and don't place it in the future. Just like anything, it's an optimization process so keep identifying the things that don't go right the first time around, make small adjustments, and the internal alignment will catch up from there. This is one of the more advanced drivers of human behavior that will really help you avoid any resistance to start living your vision.

Also, understand that your mind is full of **Mental Programming**. We are born with a computer system of a brain that is designed to keep us alive. We also install faulty programming over the years in the form of bad habits and behaviors. When a past client of mine didn't get candy as a kid and he threw a temper tantrum, the anger led him to getting what he wants. A neural pathway was created, "When I get angry, I get what I want." We used The Timeline Release Technique to find another behavior that still serves the same positive intent. We re-wrote the software program using the existing algorithms of the brain. Many past emotional events in our life cause us to behave a certain way. By utilizing these NLP techniques, this provides you the tools and abilities to reprogram your brain for optimal performance.

But in the end, it all boils down to **The Habit Loop** you fall into and the actions you take. You now understand the unconscious psychology behind habits. You may feel the dopamine rush of The Learning Loop when you learn these things and it can trick your brain to thinking you are productive. But that won't take you closer to your goals. Your thoughts create your behaviors. And your behaviors (on repeat) create your habits. Long-term habits turn into a lifestyle. And by that point, when you do these things long enough, the persistence and patience will allow you to experience Results. When you block off the neural pathways of the bad habits, build Dams and Exit Ramps, this has a direct impact on your behavior as if the programming works itself.

Ultimately, in the end, there comes a time you need to get in motion. To stop learning and to start applying this in the real world. I want to conclude this book with a famous quote by the late Billionaire founder of Apple, Steve Jobs:

You've got to find what you love. And that is as true for your work as it is for your lovers. Your work is going to fill a large part of your life, and the only way to be truly satisfied is to do what you believe is great work. And the only way to do great work is to love what you do. If you haven't found it yet, keep looking. Don't settle. As with all matters of the heart, you'll know when you find it. And, like any great relationship, it just gets better and better as the years roll on.

So keep looking until you find it. Don't settle…Your time is limited, so don't waste it living someone else's life. Don't be trapped by dogma — which is living with the results of other people's thinking. Don't let the noise of others' opinions drown out your own inner voice. And most important, have the courage to follow your heart and intuition. They somehow already know what you truly want to become. Everything else is secondary.

I wish you the best,

Andrew Alexander, Author of this book.

**SAVE 50% ON YOUR NEXT PURCHASE OR
FIRST COACHING SESSION**

**COUPON CODE:
MOTIVATION50**

Personal Development Books

Motivational Journal

Coaching

NLP Practitioner Certification

Online Video Training Program

www.DeconstructingMotivation.com

CPSIA information can be obtained
at www.ICGtesting.com
Printed in the USA
ᵀ.VHW081806080620
ᴜ57683LV00035B/3589